From a Boy to a Godly Man

A Boy's Bible Study of Joseph

From a Boy to a Godly Man
A Boy's Bible Study of Joseph
Volume II
By Katy Foster
and by Christopher Foster

Copyright © 2015 by Katy Foster and Christopher Foster
1st edition
Volume II
Printed by CreateSpace, Charleston, SC
All rights reserved.

ISBN 13: 978-1512167733
ISBN 10: 1512167738

Printed in the United States of America

From a Boy to a Godly Man

Volume II

A Boy's Bible Study of Joseph

by
Katy Leigh
Foster
&
Christopher Foster

Thank you

Hudson Grady Mauldin

&

Mia Grace Venson

for the use of your beautiful photographs to guide understanding of God's Word.

Undoubtedly, your lives will continue to touch and bless so many – you just wait and see!

For of Him and through Him and to Him are all things to whom be glory forever. Amen.

Romans 11:36

Table of Contents

Chapter 1

Your Intro

The beginning of a new Bible study is undoubtedly the beginning of a new journey in your life. You are about to focus *quite deeply* on finding truths in the Bible. This is **big** – a new journey in your life may be where God changes your life, for the rest of your life!

God has amazing plans for you, so have courage! Grasp God's glorious hand throughout this study, and watch where He points.

Joseph, the son of Jacob, is now living with God in Heaven. God wants us to know about this man. **Psalm 119:24** proclaims the reason *why* we study people of the Bible:

Your testimonies also are my delight and my counselors.
NKJV

Do you believe the words of the Bible are *a delight*? Sometimes the Bible may be hard to understand, or maybe it does not seem to give us the words that we feel we need to read right then and there. Maybe we find that some of the events recorded in the Bible are not interesting and seem to have no relevance in our lives. If reading the Bible becomes viewed as more of an *obligation* than a *pleasure,* we may discover that we honestly do not call its words a delight. So, let's change that.

Can you recall a time in your life when God's glory, power, and love were magnified in your life because you were reading your Bible? We pray that you **hunger** for His words every day, and that you **relish** and *bask* in what you read, *savoring* every word, and finding *enjoyment* and *delight*. We know with every ounce of confidence in us that you will be changed by the Bible, because we know that EVERY PERSON that hungers for His words and fills their lives with theses God-breathed words are, immediately or eventually, **changed**. We would like to prepare you and help you along the way:

Read.

Have your Bible handy. You may notice that most quotes in this study are in NKJV (New King James Version). Other Bible versions are also offered to help us grip some understanding.
Our Bible needs to be read daily. Growing up without reading the Bible is just like trying to travel in a car without tires. We go nowhere.

Apply and Obey.

Applying the Bible is living out what we read, beings doers, not just hearers. You and I cannot read the Bible as outside observers, as if it has no effect on us right here, right now. Its words are living, and they *apply* to your life today. Be ready to obey God's guidance through your Bible reading.

A huge part of applying and obeying is *memorization.* Memory verses are encouraged throughout this study. Memorizing is a great way to hide God's word in your heart. You will need a way of keeping up with your memory verses. Here are a couple of suggestions:

1. Keep all memory verses together in a stack of index cards. Punch a hole in one top corner of each card. Then, use a key ring to keep the cards together. Throughout the Bible study, write a memory verse on one of the cards. All your memory verses stay together, and this is an easy way to remember verses that you've memorized.

2. Download an app on your electronic device. Many memory verses apps are free. Just make sure you are able to include your own verses, and that you are able to use the Bible version (NKJV, NIV, KJV,...) that you prefer. A few even make it fun with different ways to memorize.

Choose either or both ways to practice memorizing your verses.

Pray.

Prayer does not have to come last, of course. Talk to God and ask Him for His guidance before you begin to read. When the study may seem difficult, tedious, or boring, just pray.

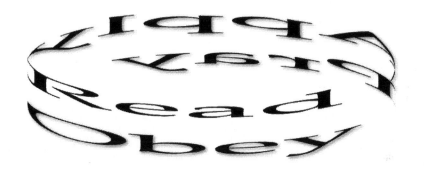

Read, apply, obey, and pray as you read God's word. It's how to read the Bible. If you practice these four steps with each Bible reading, you *will* gain a better understanding of what you have read. You *will* understand how God wants you to live. You *will* be able to make wiser choices in your life, and you *will* have a deeper and closer relationship with God. You *will* be changed, and you *will* see your Bible, the heart of our God, as a delight!

Here is further preparation for the study:

Throughout the study you will see a row of dots, like these:

· · · · ·

These dots indicate a stopping point for the day. An entire lesson does not necessarily need to be done in one day.

Stephen

The study begins with Stephen, not Joseph. Stephen lived about 4,000 years *after* Joseph. When Joseph was living, God had not only Joseph in His heart, but He also had Stephen, and He also had and has *you!*

As Joseph was sold into slavery, God already knew that his life would one day give *you* direction in your own life, and God knew it would give direction to Stephen, as you will see.

Lesson 1

Stephen

Read *Acts 6:3-15.*

Explanations in your reading:

v. 3 "…whom we may appoint over this business." NKJV, KJV

"…we will turn this responsibility over to them…"NIV

"…whom we may put in charge of this task." NASB

Describing how the church must function, many responsibilities and needs are around and within the church. A plan is made to delegate (share) these responsibilities.

v. 6 "…and laid hands on them." It does not mean they got beat up. Laying of the hands is a religious practice and symbol of receiving spiritual gifts to do God's work.

v.9 "…the Synagogue of the Freedmen…"

"…the Synagogue of the Libertines…" NKJ

A group of people who were freed by the Roman Empire from slavery that now formed their own church.

v. 12 "…the council, or Sanhedrin."

Really good word to know the meaning to! The Sanhedrin heard and decided on cases that were brought before them in their courtroom. They had a great deal of power.

Write a summary and your own thoughts of the reading:

_____

_____

_____

• • • • •

Our study starts with Stephen. Stephen loved God. He loved his church. His faith in God was practically unmatched. What a marvelous joy that pumps into the eternal heart of God when we love Him!

I imagine that the majestic eyes of God lovingly gazed at Stephen, with His glorious head turned squarely on the obedient life of Stephen. His heart washed over with joy! God greatly strengthened Stephen, so that when people saw Stephen's works, they were amazed and in awe.

However, as you could probably guess, *just like today*, there were unbelievers and enemies of God that approached Stephen and arrested him. Stephen was taken to council, which included judges, lawyers, and law enforcement – a huge majority of non-believers in Jesus Christ.

And this is to whom Stephen is expected to answer to?? How dreadful! What can he say? These are the town leaders and aristocrats that plan to glare at Stephen with their noses turned up. He was wrongly accused of blasphemy, and all these enemies are staring at him in disgust…until something happens, and what they see is amazing!

Verse 15 tells us that the councilmen are staring at Stephen because his face shown like an angel!

What did that look like? I am not really sure. I do not recall ever seeing an angel, but I do know that it was awesome! Possibly bright, glowing, maybe even shining inflamed, like lightning!

I imagine those men stared, with big round eyes about to pop out of their heads, and their chins dropped so low that some of them probably had to pick their chins up off the floor!

Apply & Obey
by Chris

"Therefore, brethren, seek out from among you seven men of good reputation, full of the Holy Spirit and wisdom, whom we may appoint over business."

Acts 6:3

As men, whether we know it or not, we define ourselves by *what we do* for a living. One of the first questions a man will ask of another upon meeting for the first time is, "so what do you do for a living?" meaning "what kind of job do you have?"

Work ethic, as defined by Merriam-Webster, is a belief in work as a moral good. Ultimately, we are working for the Lord, so what we do should support and enhance the greater moral good in our society. Colossians 3:23-24 says, *"And whatever you do, do it heartily, as to the Lord and not to men, knowing that from the Lord you will receive the reward of the inheritance; for you serve the Lord Christ."* Therefore, *how* we work is more important than *where* we work.

Now, you may have jobs, or tasks, where you ask yourself, "How am I  working for the Lord here?" I had one of those jobs. Katy and I had been married for one year when I found out that the company I was working for was downsizing. In other words, I was losing my job. We were in a new house, were pregnant with our first child, and I needed a job fast. I was offered a position at a water treatment plant within a poultry facility. One word describes this job, and that is *"disgusting!"* Basically, I was cleaning the water that was used to scold the chicken's feathers off before they were eventually killed and put on your dinner plate. Don't get me wrong, I love fried chicken as much as the next person, but the job was nasty!

So, you may ask, how was I serving the Lord in that job? Well, I wasn't doing the job for myself or greed, but I was doing the job for my family. In the First Book of Timothy 5:8, Paul says, "But if anyone does not provide for his own, and especially for those of his household, he has denied the faith and is worse than an unbeliever." Those are powerful words that say we are to give our all to whatever job the Lord has chosen for us to do.

Stephen's job before being appointed is unknown; yet, whatever he did, he did heartily for the Lord. Joseph, as you will soon read, also had jobs that some might say were disgusting or revolting. But ultimately, he knew he was working for God, and this was exemplified in his work ethic. Genesis 39:2, "The Lord was with Joseph, and he was a successful man."

So, you may ask, "How does this all apply to me? I'm not even old enough to have a job." Developing a strong work ethic does not happen overnight, but it begins when you are young. Starting every task we are given by first asking "How will this task work to serve the Lord and others?" This will put you well on your way to developing a strong work ethic. *Give it to God first*, and He will guide you the rest of the way.

Look up **Colossians 3:23**, and write the verse below:

_____

_____

_____

Memorize the verse, and add it to your memory verses list.

Dear Heavenly Father,
What amazing things You do for
those who love You! Thank you for showing
me how loving You are through Your Word;
You were always with Stephen, and
You are always with me.
Amen.

Lesson 2

Share the Good News

Read *Acts 7:1-9.*

Write a summary and your own thoughts of the reading:

_____

_____

_____

· · · · ·

The high priest nervously stands to face and question an angelic glowing Stephen, shining bright. Most likely, the knees of the high priest were shaking so hard they knocked together. As he asks Stephen a question, I imagine his voice was shaking as bad as his knees. He asks, "Aaaare th, th, th, these th, th, th, things s, s, so?"

Now, Stephen could have responded with a thought of defeat, thinking, "What's the use? They're not going to believe me."

However, precious brothers in Christ, Stephen did not respond in his own strength. Through the Holy Spirit, he rested his weary mind on the Scriptures, and on all those already written about (Abraham, Jacob, Joseph, Moses, Joshua, David) that *persevered* through tough times, and kept loving the Lord. Therefore, Stephen just could not help himself but to share God's marvelous history and great works. Stephen proclaimed great passages from the Bible that he had hid in his own heart.

Stephen tells these leaders of the court about men that lived for God, beginning with Abraham.

In verse 9, Stephen begins sharing the life of Joseph.

Perhaps as a growing boy, like you, Stephen studied Joseph to the same extent that you are preparing to do now. I believe Stephen considered that his own life should be a reflection of Joseph's life, which greatly reflected the life of our Savior Jesus Christ.

Dear Heavenly Father,
Thank You for being our
Guide and our Creator, the Creator
of Joseph, and the Creator of us. Speak to us
through Your Word.
Amen.

Lesson 3
Stephen and You

Read Acts 6:3.

Stephen also studied the Book of Genesis and the history of Joseph; therefore, there were particular times that Stephen thought about Joseph.

The church needed leaders that had a good reputation, full of the Holy Spirit and of wisdom. They chose seven men, and Stephen was one of them.

A Good Reputation...

A good reputation means to be known by others to be good, and to be known for doing what is right. A good reputation means you have a past of being honest, dependable, and a good servant. It does not mean that everybody likes you. It means you are pleasing God above yourself or others.

By reading about Joseph, Stephen knew that Joseph persevered through the loneliness and trials; therefore, Joseph upheld a good reputation. He *chose* to uphold a good reputation:

> "A good name is to be chosen rather than great riches."
>
> Proverbs 22:1

Stephen had his own trials when he chose to do right. We will feel lonely and disliked sometimes for choosing to please God instead of others; but as you grow, remember, you are building a good reputation.

Read the following verse, then copy:
He must increase, but I must decrease. John 3:30

_____

_____

Memorize this verse, and add it to your memory verses list.

Let us now grasp God's hand and lay our eyes on the same Bible verses of Joseph that Stephen once did.

Dear Heavenly Father,
Thank You for being the Name
Above All Names! May I uphold a good
name and reputation, as is
Your will.
Amen.

Chapter 2

Set the Stage

Jumping right into Joseph's story is bound to leave us confused and thinking. "…Who?...what?.... who again?..."

Quite a few people are mentioned and involved, with so much history behind each one. The information is not going to make much sense without taking a moment to look at it. All is found in the Book of Genesis.

Knowing more information helps us from jumping to wrong conclusions when we read what Joseph, Jacob, or a brother did next.

The chapter starts with a family tree for you to fill out. Use the information on page 13 to fill in the family tree.

Start at the bottom blank of the family tree with the name Abraham.

This will be a good chapter to bookmark so that you can refer back to it when you find yourself asking "…Who…what…who?" There are many people mentioned in the life of Joseph.

Family Tree of Joseph

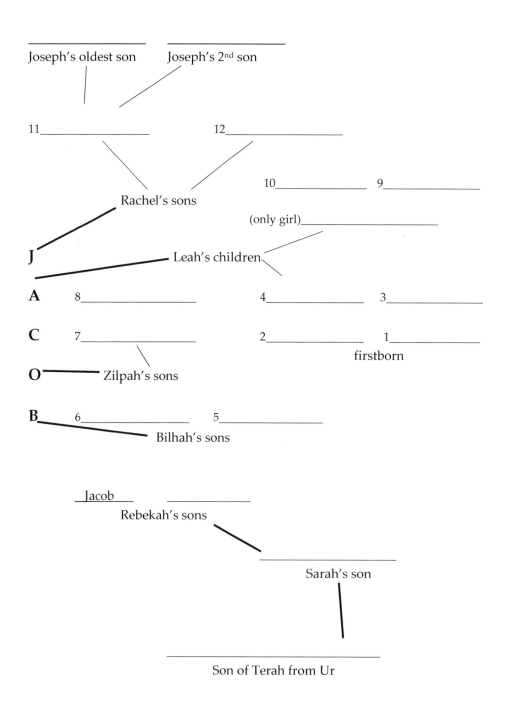

Joseph's oldest son   Joseph's 2nd son

11_____   12_____

10_____   9_____

Rachel's sons

(only girl)_____

J

Leah's children

A   8_____   4_____   3_____

C   7_____   2_____   1_____

firstborn

O————Zilpah's sons

B___ 6_____   5_____

Bilhah's sons

_Jacob___ _____

Rebekah's sons

Sarah's son

_____

Son of Terah from Ur

Here is a historical summary of Joseph's descendants:

Abraham, Josephs' great-grandfather, was married to Sarah, and their son was Isaac.

Isaac, Joseph's grandfather, married Rebekah, and they had twins, Jacob and Esau.

Jacob, Joseph's father, married two sisters, Leah and Rachel. Jacob had twelve sons and one daughter, by both wives, and his wives' two maidservants, named Bilhah and Zilpah. Therefore, Jacob was the father of thirteen children (which includes Joseph) involving four mothers – Leah, Rachel, Bilhah, and Zilpah.

Leah gave birth to his firstborn child named Reuben. Then three more children, Simeon, Levi, and Judah.

Then by Leah's given maidservant Bilhah were born Dan and Naphtali.

From Rachel's given maidservant Zilpah were born Gad and Asher.

Leah then gave birth to three more children, first Issachar, then Zebulun, and her last child was Jacob's only girl, Dinah.

Finally, Rachel gave birth to Joseph. She died giving birth to Joseph's youngest brother and her last child Benjamin.

The Children of Israel (Jacob):

As you read your Bible and come to a name, particularly one of Joseph's brothers' names, you can come back to these pages to fill in the information you learn about each brother. (Joseph's name is not included.)

Reuben_____

_____

Simeon_____

_____

Levi_____

_____

Judah_____

_____

Dan_____

_____

Naphtali_____

_____

Gad_____

_____

Asher_____

_____

Issachar_____

_____

Zebulun_____

_____

Dinah_____

_____

Benjamin_____

_____

Chapter 3

Completely Covered

Genesis 37

Understand that as you read your Bible and pray, God is not just with you, but He is guiding you, loving you, teaching you, molding you, and preparing you for His will.

There is nothing in your life that will be more satisfying, more joyous, and more beautiful than allowing God to work through you.

I believe the hands of God will work wonders in *your* life, because your life is precious to Him. Through His Son, Jesus Christ, you are completely covered!

Lesson 1

A Bit Tense

Read *Genesis 37:1-4.*

Explanations in your reading:

v. 1 "...where his father was a stranger..." KJV, NKJV

"...where his father had sojourned..." NAS

"...where his father had stayed..." NIV

Although Jacob's father Isaac was born in Canaan, Jacob's grandfather Abraham was from Ur, in the Mesopotamia. Canaan is the new land given to them by God.

v. 2 "...Joseph brought a bad report of them to his father..."NKJV, NAS, NIV

"...Joseph brought unto his father their evil report." KJV

The Bible does not tell us exactly what it was that the four brothers did; however, whatever they did bothered Joseph enough to feel it needed to be made known to his father. This verse gives us a good indication that Joseph was a good boy, and also close to his father.

Write a summary and your own thoughts of the reading:

_____

_____

_____

• • • • •

Unless you wrote it above in your summary, may I be the first to say, "Talk about an earful!" These first four verses in Genesis 37 give a flood of family information!

Apply...

Fill in the blanks to get a better perspective of it all:

How old is Joseph as our lesson begins? _____

What is the sons' chore, and the family's primary occupation?
_____

What are the four brothers' names that are with Joseph in the field?

_____   _____

_____   _____

Are these brothers of Joseph of noble, righteous character out in the field?
_____

Jacob was not only a shepherd. He was also skilled at another trade.
What was it?
_____
_____

Verse 3 tells us that Jacob loved Joseph more than any of his other sons.
What is your reaction to that?

_____

Israel (Jacob) also makes and gives Joseph a tunic, a robe with lots of expensive colors on it. This not only was expensive, and probably cost a nice chunk of Jacob's flock or other goods to pay for the colorful material, but it took much time to make a complete coat.

Imagine your parents telling you,…

"That big delicious piece of cake is not for you! It is for your darling brother. You can lick his plate when he's done."

Now, let me ask you; are you going to turn your head to lovingly smile at your brother and say, "That's wonderful, bro. Enjoy your cake."???

I simply doubt it. Although your brother did not do anything wrong, a bit of tension and uneasiness may build up between the two of you.

Now add on, in your imagination, that this same brother, full of delicious cake, is tattling on you! How are you going to react?...

This is NOT a parenting Bible study; therefore, we are not focusing on what Israel, the father, should and should not do.

You and I cannot control what others do. We can try to help, give great advice, ask them to stop doing something, and we can pray for others. But, *we cannot control* what others do. We can only take responsibility for what *we* do, how we respond, and the choices we make.

Joseph's brothers fell short here. They *chose* to hate their own brother.

So, what are we to do when feelings of anger or jealously arise in us? The Bible gives us guidance.

Read the following verses from the Book of James here or in your own Bible:

But if you have bitter envy and self-seeking in your hearts, do not boast and lie against the truth. v15 This wisdom does not descend from above, but is earthly, sensual, demonic. v16 For where envy and self-seeking exist, confusion and every evil thing are there. v17 But the wisdom that is from above is first pure, then peaceable, gentle, willing to yield, full of mercy and good fruits, without partiality and without hypocrisy.

James 3:14-17

These first three verses explain *what we need to get rid of* that may be in our hearts:

BITTERNESS: it comes from *not* getting what we want, and pouting and feeling sorry for ourselves. Get rid of it!

ENVY: wishing we had what others have. Get rid of it!

SELF-SEEKING: wanting what I want without caring about what others may want or need. Putting me first. Me, me, me. Get rid of it!

BOASTING: Bragging about how great I am and the great things I have done. Get rid of it!

LYING: Being dishonest, especially so we can keep boasting. Get rid of it!

Circle any of the above sins that may be in your heart. Write a prayer asking God to help rid you of the sin(s) you circled:

_____

_____

_____

_____

_____

Verse 17 gives us hope. Write **James 3:17** from your own Bible in the space below, and memorize.

_____

_____

_____

_____

_____

Once memorized, add this verse to your memory verses list.

Dear Heavenly Father,
Thank you for being my Teacher, showing
me how to make peace with the people in my
life. I love you. In the name of Jesus,
Amen.

Lesson 2

Dreamland

Read *Genesis 37:5-11.*

Explanations in your reading:

v.7 "…binding sheaves…my sheaf…" Gathering and bundling together wheat.

v. 11 Dad confronts Joseph, aware that Jacob himself, along with his father Isaac, and his grandfather Abraham, all had wonderful close relationships with God. Jacob may have wondered, "Are these dreams from God?"

Write a summary and your own thoughts of the reading:

_____

_____

_____

• • • • •

If someone says to you, "Hey, I had a dream that you bowed down to me. Yep. It's true…"

…So, in hearing those words being said to you, would your reaction be similar to the reactions of Joseph's brothers? Most likely, yes.

Joseph already knew his brothers hated him. Why did he feel the need to share this dream with them?

Let's go back in time so we can get a new perspective. Two essential facts will change the way you read about Joseph:

#1: First of all, any and all quiet time that Joseph had with God included no Bible! *No Bible!* The Book of Genesis had not even yet been written. Moses wrote the Book of Genesis after the exodus from Egypt, over 300 years after Joseph had already died!

Now, it is not that Joseph had no written documentation. He may have had some type of written records. However, and more importantly, Joseph had multiple conversations with his father Israel (Jacob), and as a young boy he was blessed to hear his grandfather Isaac speak of *his* relationship with God. Joseph had precious moments of his life to hear first-hand about his great-grandfather Abraham. The relationships between Joseph and his father and grandfather had to have been really strong as they shared their experiences with God. Joseph, grasping on to every word, was learning more about God and growing closer to Him.

Can you imagine what it was like at dinner time, having conversations with Jacob and Isaac about their talks with God? Imagine Jacob sitting around at dinner with his sons, and he remarks, "Yep. I'll never forget that wrestling match. You boys want to hear about it?" (if interested, see Genesis 32:24-32 – *really* good reading!) Then maybe Grandfather Isaac replies, "Aw, that's nothing! My dad Abraham almost turned me into a sacrifice!" (see Genesis 22:1-14)

Joseph may not have had God's Holy Word, like we do today; however, he had the *actual people* that we read about sitting with him!

Yet, as Joseph's father and grandfather pointed out (and as Joseph will learn), God WILL do amazing things in our lives, so be ready!

#2: Now for the second point,… A dream from God?!? How is Joseph to respond? What does he do? What does he say? Joseph must have been thinking, "My brothers who hate me?...Bowing down to me?... As if they respect me?...And love me?...And don't hate me?...What is the purpose of such a dream?...Is God giving me prophecy, showing me His will?..."

? ? ? ?

These are HUGE thoughts for Joseph. He could not keep it in, and he told his brothers. Verse 8 tells us that the brothers then hated Joseph even more. They did not believe him.

The brothers never viewed Joseph's dreams as testimony into God's will. They viewed Joseph's dreams as Joseph being boastful and full of himself.

Apply and Obey

Should we keep quiet of God's will so that we do not offend anyone? Absolutely NEVER. Here is why:

Offending people at the name of Jesus is inevitable – a done deal. People *will* be offended. It *is* going to happen. Not every time, of course. As a matter of fact, many times, and *most* of the times, when you speak of Jesus, you may be surprised to see how many people are spiritually hungry and *want* to hear what you have to say about Jesus. But, there will be other times when you may notice that when you say Jesus, it makes people feel uncomfortable. This is because there is so much power in just His name alone!

Beliefs in other gods, such as Buddha or Allah, do not get the same response. However, say the name of Jesus, and there is a sense of majesty in the midst. After all, you just said the name "JESUS." My sweet brother, it is a powerful name.

PROCLAIM HIS LOVE! And do not worry! God the Spirit is right there to help you! Saying one sentence, just a few words, just may be all a person needs to hear to turn their lives to Jesus.

Look up **1 Peter 3:15**, and copy the verse below:

_____

_____

_____

_____

_____

_____

Memorize this verse and share the verse with someone. Also, add this verse to your memory verses list.

• • • • •

Read the above verse again. The Bible revision called "The Message," gives us 1 Peter 3:13-18 in this way:

"If with heart and soul you're doing good, do you think you can be stopped? Even if you suffer for it, you're still better off. Don't give the opposition a second thought. Through thick and thin, keep your hearts at attention, in adoration before Christ, your Master. Be ready to speak up and tell anyone who asks why you're living the way you are, and always with the utmost courtesy. Keep a clear conscience before God so that when people throw mud at you, none of it will stick. They'll end up realizing that they're the ones who need a bath. It's better to suffer for doing good, if that's what God wants, than to be punished for doing bad. That's what Christ did definitively: suffered because of others' sins, the Righteous One for the unrighteous ones. He went through it all—was put to death and then made alive—to bring us to God."

What if God plans to put an unbeliever in your path -- what would you like to say that shows God's love for them and your love for them? Or, pretend you are writing a letter to this person…

Here are some suggestions for what to say:

- You could share information about your own relationship with God – what you love about it, and what may be difficult.

- Share some Bible verses that you have learned and like.
- Share what it means to be saved.
- Ask how you can pray for him/her.
- Explain how much God loves him/her.

This is a huge step in preparing to be a witness and a shining light for Jesus!

Write down some ideas here:

_____

_____

_____

_____

_____

_____

_____

_____

_____

_____

_____

Like Joseph, we do not have to be quiet when it comes to God's will.

Dear Heavenly Father,
Thank You for teaching and guiding us.
We asked dear Lord that You help prepare
us to be Your witnesses.
Amen.

Reflection of Jesus

Use Your Gifts!

Dad (Jacob) openly showed Joseph more love, and Joseph's brothers hated him. What did Joseph do? He accepted the loving gift of the tunic from his father, and he wore it. He was seventeen, and well aware that his dad made a beautiful coat *only* for him.

This is so crucially important to understand: Joseph chose to wear the coat proudly, gratefully, and even around his brothers,…and he chose *correctly!*

You might be thinking, "Maybe Joseph should not have worn the coat around his brothers so that they would not become angry," or "Joseph should have shared the coat," or "Joseph should not have shown the coat to his brothers. He should have kept it a secret."

Joseph's response to receiving the gift was the best response. He received a gift from his father because he loved, honored, and obeyed his father, just as God's perfect will wanted him to.

Throughout the gospels (Matthew, Mark, Luke, and John), the Pharisees continuously plot and show their hate for Jesus.

*Then the Pharisees and Sadducees came, and **testing** Him…
Matthew 16:1*

*Then the Pharisees came out and began to **dispute** with Him,…Mark 8:11*

*The Pharisees also came to Him, **testing** Him,… Matthew 19:3*

*Then the Pharisees went and **plotted** how they might **entangle** Him in His talk. Matthew 22:15*

*So they **watched** Him, and sent spies who pretended to be righteous, that they might **seize** on His words, in order to **deliver** Him to the power and the authority of the governor.*
Luke 20:20

Although Jesus was rejected, hated, despised, and disrespected, He continued to share God's love, to teach, to heal, and to rebuke.

Jesus could have chosen not to share salvation with others in order to keep peace with the powerful Pharisees. He could have kept it a secret, but that was not God's will, was it?

Whether the Pharisees or anyone else liked it or not, Jesus proclaimed in John 14:6,

"I am the way, the truth, and the life.

No one comes to the Father

except through Me."

How horrible if the hate of the Pharisees overpowered Jesus's teachings and guidance into eternal life. Love is more powerful, and love is honest.

How horrible it would have been if the hate of Joseph's brothers overpowered his respect and submission to his father Jacob. Love is more powerful, and love is honest.

Reflection of You

Your Heavenly Father has some wonderful gifts for you. God's gifts, like a coat of many colors, are out of his deep love for you. His gifts are good and perfect.

33

His greatest gift to you is to live forever with Him. Your response is hopefully to accept this gift. How? By loving Him and by giving Him every day of your life, because you understand that you are not perfect, and you just cannot ever get it completely right; therefore, surrender those heavy chains to Jesus Christ. He bore the burden of your sin. Take His hands by making Him Lord of your life. Accept this gift from God out of your love for Him.

Daily, God tops off this gift of eternity with other gifts to equip you to do His work. He also gives you more gifts because He loves you.

These gifts should be used, and never hidden, to show your love for God and to bring glory to Him.

Please write out one of my favorite verses from your own Bible, **Romans 11:36:**

_____

_____

_____

Memorize this verse and add it to your memory verses list.

Have you received the gift of Jesus Christ as the Lord of your life and as the bearer of all your sins, acknowledging Him as your Savior from death (loaded question, think about it)? _____

Are you allowing your gifts from God to shine and strengthen?

Check an answer(s) for each gift:

	I am using	I need to	I will start
Daily prayer time	_____	_____	_____
Daily Bible reading	_____	_____	_____
Loving others	_____	_____	_____
Forgiving others	_____	_____	_____
Honoring parents	_____	_____	_____
Exercising	_____	_____	_____
Eating healthy	_____	_____	_____
Attending church	_____	_____	_____
Sharing God's love	_____	_____	_____
Excelling in schoolwork	_____	_____	_____
Using special talents/skills	_____	_____	_____

Are there any other gifts from God that you can strengthen for Him?

_____

_____

God loves you so much. Like Jesus and Joseph, proudly show others God's love.

*Dear Heavenly Father,
Thank You for being LOVE!
I love you! Thank You for giving
Your Son to die in my place. Thank
You for loving me. Guide me by Your Holy
Spirit to share this love. In
Jesus' name, Amen.*

Lesson 3
"The Pits"

Read *Genesis 37:12-24.*

Explanations in your reading:

v. 13   "Here I am." NKJV, "am I" KJV

"Very well," NIV

"I will go." NAS

Powerful quote of a child to his father. Joseph assures his father that he will obey and serve him.

Dothan and Shechem:

Shechem is in the land of Canaan, and was bought by Jacob. With my own calculations, Dothan is about 12 miles north of Shechem. So it is not as if the brothers wanted to stop by Dothan for a couple of hours. It took longer than a couple of hours just to walk there. Perhaps they were going to trade goods, or to find food.

Distance between Shechem and Hebron:

Approximately 30 miles. He may have walked 5 to 10 miles per day; therefore the trip may have taken Joseph 3 to 6 days to get to Shechem. Then another day or two to get to Dothan.

The Pits: So, where are all these pits coming from? Could I be running and playing outside and suddenly fall into a pit? Some translations use the word "cistern." A cistern worked as a water supply for fields, in which a hole is dug into the ground to catch and hold rainwater, to be used for animals and crops.

v. 23   In stealing Joseph's coat, the brothers disrespected their father. They disvalued something that was created by their father.

Write a summary and your own thoughts of the reading:

_____

_____

_____

_____

• • • • •

Reuben has another plan. However, he is outnumbered by several angry, hateful brothers.

Reuben planned to take Joseph home to his father, as a gift almost. Was Reuben not angry with Joseph, like the rest of the brothers? Possibly. However, Reuben carried in his heart honor for his father. Reuben thought, 'Little Brother Joseph does drive me absolutely crazy sometimes, but Dad loves him so much. I know it would break Dad's heart if Joseph was killed.' Reuben's plan was to *temporarily* make the brothers happy by *always* keeping his father happy.

Read
Apply
Obey
Pray

Apply & Obey
by Chris

The words "Here I am" spoken by Joseph in Genesis 37:13 can be applicable to our daily lives as young men of God. Little did Joseph know at the time that his words would ultimately lead him on a life-long journey of gripping tightly to God's loving hand.

Answering selflessly when we are called can be difficult at times to do. Approaching your mom and dad, and God, with the words, "Here I am," shows faith in their guidance to you, and your love for them as leaders in your life. Approaching others with the words, "Here I am," shows humility, confidence, and selflessness, like Jesus. Normally, when we are called upon it is because someone needs or wants something from us. And many times we are selfishly unwilling to answer the call.

For us, as men, humbly answering the call, whether it be from our parents, or from the Lord, or anyone else, will take the focus off of us and put it on others just as Jesus did on the cross for us.

Look up **Genesis 37:13** in your Bible, and write the *last sentence of the verse* below:

_____

_____

_____

Memorize this verse, and add to your memory verses list.

Dear Heavenly Father,
Thank You for being Merciful.
Help me to also show mercy and
to love others.
Amen.

Lesson 4
Tribulations

Read *Genesis 37:25-36.*

Explanations in your reading:

v. 25   *Ishmaelites and Midianites.* From the families of Ishmael and 28 Midian, who were half-brothers, and Abraham's sons. Ishmael's family grew in the area of Egypt and the Wilderness of Paran. The Midianites seem to have settled more in the southeast region of the Red Sea. The Ishmaelites and the Midianites, in the Book of Genesis, may be the same group of people. You can find these places on your map.

v. 27   Judah gives the suggestion to sell Joseph. Pretty big suggestion! Nonetheless, his listening little brothers comply.

v. 28   *"Twenty shekels of silver."* Twenty pieces of silver used as currency/money. Also, the brothers kept Joseph's coat, so Joseph was left wearing very little.

v. 29   Apparently, Reuben was nowhere around when Joseph was sold.

v. 30   *"Where shall I go?"* NKJV *"Where can I turn?"* NIV
Reuben does not know how to find Joseph, and he knows his father Jacob is going to be so upset, Reuben is now overcome with dread in having to face his father.

v. 32- What an evil lie to their own father! What horrible sadness
35   and depression they allow their own father to endure!

v. 36   Potiphar is an important Egyptian political figure.

Write a summary and your own thoughts of the reading:

_____

_____

_____

•   •   •   •   •

Apply & Obey
by Chris

Joseph grew up with these brothers and loved them. The pain of how little they loved him back had to have been hard to bear. He is now possibly tied up by the Ishmaelites and forced to walk long distances without stopping. He was a loyal, obedient son, yet his whole life has changed. What was he thinking about as he was carried off, not knowing where he was being taken? I imagine he was thinking about his dad Jacob, still at home waiting for Joseph's return; and about his mom Rachel, who died when Joseph was a young boy, possibly eight years old.

Joseph may have also been confused about why this was happening to him. He was a good son. He shared prophecy of God, and now his life seemed to have hit a dead end.

However, I believe Joseph never lost his faith or hope in the Lord. Although I never have had to endure the kind of persecution that Joseph endured, there were times as a young man that I was scared and experienced some pretty rough times by my peers.

Read
Apply
Obey
Pray

When I was in the eighth grade, we moved into a new home. Up until that time, I had the opportunity to attend a Christian school, and had many friends.

This new move would require a major school change. I would have to attend public school! The thought of public school didn't scare me at first, but little did I know what I was in for.

40

For an eighth grader, I was small in stature, and this would be used against me throughout my eighth grade year. Although long forgiven, to this day, I can remember his name, his cowboy boots, and the strong stench of tobacco in his mouth. He also had a tendency to not be very

nice, especially to me, the new kid on the block. I *vividly* remember those experiences in eighth grade, and I remember conversations I had with my parents about my experiences. I remember talking to God and asking Him why, but I also remember the sense of peace that the Lord gave me in those times of trials. **Romans 5:3-5** speaks to the hope we can have in the Lord when enduring tribulations in our lives:

And not only that, but we also glory in tribulations, knowing that tribulation produces perseverance and perseverance produces character, hope. Now hope does not disappoint poured out in our hearts by the Holy Spirit who was given to us.
Romans 5:3-5

More than likely, any rough times, or even persecutions, that we will endure in life will pale in comparison to what Joseph had to endure. But, our response to God should be the same, and that is that we should lean on Him during these times. As God's children, when we do suffer (*and we will*), God is with us and He will never leave us, nor will He ever forget about us.

In the middle of the storms that come in your life, remember that God has a plan, a beautiful, glorious plan. I've seen it myself.

Look up **Jeremiah 29:11**, and copy the verse below:

_____

_____

_____

_____

Commit to memorizing this verse, and hide it in your heart – you *will* need this verse one day and many days!

Dear Heavenly Father,
Thank You for being our Father
that will never leave us or forget about us.
May we always remember Your presence
on tough days.
Amen.

Chapter 4
God's Powerful Presence
Genesis 39

I think we both understand that the thirty-seventh chapter of Genesis that we just completed could have been read in one night, instead of being divided up into days and days of reading. However, it is so important that we understand that, along with learning more about Joseph, we are learning *how* to read the Bible. It is a bit different from reading a fiction chapter book from the library. In fiction books, you are the audience, a bystander, an on-looker. However, with the Bible, you are one of the characters. You are there, and this is real. The same God that you read about is the exact same God that is with you *right now!* When you think about it, that's really cool!

We can get the most out of God's Word by applying it in our lives, obeying God's guidance and commands, and praying about what we read. Try not to consider this as work, because the Holy Spirit will guide you; consequently, your "work" at studying the Bible will be rewarding.

Please notice that this next chapter that we are reading is Genesis 39, and NOT Genesis 38: we are skipping Genesis 38. Genesis 38 focuses on Joseph's brother Judah, and not Joseph. The chapter is actually pretty amazing – it explains how Judah is a descendant of Jesus Christ. Chapter 38 is included on my website. To stay focused on Joseph, **continue your Bible reading to Genesis 39.**

Lesson 1:
God is Right Here

Read *Genesis 39:1-4.*

Write a summary and your own thoughts of the reading:

_____

_____

_____

•　　•　　•　　•　　•

Verse three explains that Potiphar *saw* that God was with Joseph. How did the master see this? Possibly by the way Joseph acted, or by the things he said.

What do you think Joseph did for the master to *see* that God was with him? Here are some possibilities:

- Potiphar noticed that Joseph was **honest**;
- Joseph **showed gratitude**, even though he was a servant;
- Joseph was **not lazy**;
- Joseph did **not argue**;
- Joseph did **not complain**;
- Potiphar may have seen Joseph **praying** to God;
- Potiphar heard **words of great wisdom** that Joseph spoke;
- Joseph was **kind**;
- Joseph was **respectful** to his master;
- Joseph **never joined in any gossip**;
- Joseph was **humble**.

The Holy Spirit will guide us to strengthen all these traits. Are there any traits here that you feel the Holy Spirit is wanting to strengthen in you right now? Circle any, as you feel led.

Potiphar *saw* that God was with Joseph. The verse does not say that Potiphar was *told* that God was with Joseph. The verse also does not say that Joseph *told* Potiphar God was with him. Joseph never said, "Hey, Potiphar, I'm a great guy. I've really got it going on. God is with me." Joseph never said that. No one said it. Potiphar just knew it, because he could tell by what he saw and by what he observed.

Apply & Obey
by Chris

Integrity! It is what you are when no one is looking. In other words, your thoughts, actions, and attitude should be pleasing to the Lord at all times, not only when you are around others. It is easy for us as men to portray ourselves as one way when we are around others, only to change our actions dramatically when we think we are alone. However, if you are a firm believer in Christ, you know that *you are never alone*, but that Christ is always with us. So, if showing integrity is important to us when we are physically around others, then it should be equally as important when we are alone with the Lord.

Being a man of integrity can also help alleviate the pain of rejection, which we experience as we grow in our walk with God. The Bible is full of examples of Godly men who experienced rejection, e.g. Jesus, Joseph, David, Paul. But each of these gentlemen had a high level of integrity, and living by this high moral code allowed them to persevere and withstand the pain of rejection.

Since we are all men of the flesh, our integrity needs to be kept in check. **Philippians 4:8** is a verse to keep close to your heart as you grow in your walk and integrity:

Finally, brethren, whatever things are true, whatever things are noble, whatever things are just, whatever things are pure, whatever things are lovely, whatever things are of good report, if there is any virtue and if there is anything praiseworthy-meditate on these things.

Now look up **Colossians 3:23**, and copy the verse below.

_____

_____

_____

Memorize the verse, and add it to your memory verses list.

Dear Heavenly Father,
Thank You for always seeing us,
Never casting us away. You are our
Strength and Guide to please
You, O Lord.
Amen.

Lesson 2:

Girls!

Read *Genesis 39:5-20.*

Write a summary and your own thoughts of the reading:

_____

_____

_____

. . . . .

Joseph has impressed Potiphar, and he is given complete authority over everything. God loves Joseph, Potiphar loves Joseph, and Potiphar's wife seems to think she loves Joseph, too!

A word (or more) about girls...

Girls are a wonderful blessing to the world God created. Girls are beautiful, kind-spirited, fun, graceful, and just lovely. Girls, and boys, unfortunately, are also favorite "tools" that the devil likes to use.

Now, I did not say that girls and boys are evil or satanic. The truth is that Satan delights in turning YOU away from God with *anything* that can get your attention, including a girl.

The Bible tells of women who walk away from God and cause a man to fall:

Eve: (Genesis 3:6) She gave the forbidden fruit to Adam.

Job's wife: (Job 2:9) She encouraged Job to "Curse God and
die!"

Delilah: (Judges 16:19) She shaved Samson's head, and
allowed him to be taken prisoner by the Philistines.

Bathsheba: (II Samuel 11:2) She precariously takes her bath
outside as if no one can see her, consequently enticing
King David.

And also, Potiphar's wife.

Time and time again in the Bible, God shows us how and why we must not lose our footing, being swept away, way off God's way. **Self-control** keeps you from acting on any emotions you may feel, helps to keep thoughts from *growing*, and will help you leave that tempting situation.

In fairness, there are many amazing godly women in the Bible as well. Women such as Hannah, Esther, Mary, Elizabeth, Priscilla, and Mary Magdalene did not cause anyone to sin, but encouraged others to love God.

Apply & Obey
by Chris

Temptation, the reason for the fall of man. This thorn of life has been with us since the beginning of time, and will always be there tapping us on the shoulder pressuring us to walk in the opposite direction that God intends for us to walk.

Although Joseph was a slave in Egypt, he was viewed highly by Potiphar, and was given the job of overseeing his entire house. In that house was Potiphar's wife.

As a young man, by now, you are beginning to notice the beauty of a woman. The woman was created by God to complete man; and she does, *only* when man views her in the way God intended her to be viewed – HIS creation, preparing for HIS will.

Now, Joseph was heavily tempted by Potiphar's wife, but he knew that if he gave into this temptation that it would be a sin against God. So, he did the best thing that he could have done in that situation, and that is to get up and leave! Although he suffered physically for making this choice, *he did not suffer spiritually* in his relationship with God. Actually, his self-control allowed the relationship with God to grow.

We are all tempted on a daily basis, and some temptations are big and some will be small. Sometimes you will be alone when temptation strikes, and sometimes you will be with others. Wherever and however, how do you *respond* to the temptation?

Read
Apply
Obey
Pray

Joseph overcame the temptation. In Genesis 39:12 the Bible tells us, "she caught him by his garment, saying, 'Lie with me.' But he left his garment in her hand, and fled and ran outside."

How Joseph responded to temptation thousands of years ago is how we need to respond when we are tempted:

You will find that although sometimes difficult, the Holy Spirit will guide you with discernment and a *pull*. Leaving the scene of temptation and resisting temptation will support you in your growth as the man that God intends you to be.

Keep God close to you, run from temptation, just as Joseph did, and be "bold" in your self-control!

Look up **Proverbs 4:23**, and copy the verse below:

_____

_____

_____

Memorize the verse, and add it to your memory verses list.

Dear Heavenly Father,
Thank You for being Truth.
We pray that the girl that You
are preparing for marriage of the
young man reading this is walking in
Your will right now.
Amen.

Lesson 3:
"Woe is Me!"

Read *Genesis 39:21-23.*

Write a summary and your own thoughts of the reading:

_____

_____

_____

. . . . .

Joseph just cannot seem to catch a break. Drama to the left, drama to the right. He did absolutely nothing wrong, and ended up in prison.

Apply & Obey

Look up **1 Thessalonians 5:18**, and write the verse here:

_____

_____

_____

_____

Memorize this verse, and add to your memory verses list.

The verse instructs us to give thanks in everything. In *EVERYTHING??* How can I give thanks in everything? In particular, how can I be thankful for "setbacks" (we'll call them) in life, meaning those things that may be in our lives that we wish were *not* in our lives.

We will take, for example, homework. There are so many other things you could be doing, but you must figure out fractions, and variables, and mathematical formulas.   How, oh how, can we give thanks for homework?

Well, I suppose we should practice God's command now.   We realize homework is important.   It gives us *knowledge*, and it *strengthens our obedience* to our teacher. We learn *perseverance* as we try to find answers. Really, the more we think about it, the list seems to just go on and on of what you gain from homework. So take the time to thank God for homework *now*. Still not convinced, huh? I will help:

Dear Heavenly Father,

It is hard for me to be thankful for something that I do not like, such as homework, but I understand that it helps me become smarter and stronger.   Therefore, thank you for homework, and the chance for me to obey You by doing my homework. Amen.

.   .   .   .   .

Another "setback" to giving thanks in everything in our day may be when having to face consequences, which means we got in trouble.   We received a finger pointing at us, or a disapproving look, or we were told that what we did was wrong, bad, and we *are* guilty.   What a horrible feeling, right? Nonetheless, the Bible says to give thanks for everything.   But for getting into trouble?

As hard as it may be when you are in trouble, thank God for the leadership and authority in your life. Thanking God will help keep you from having the wrong thoughts about authority, particularly your parents.

Considering we are all born in sin, it is easier sometimes to react in a sinful nature by thinking, *"my parents just don't understand,"* or *"my parents don't love me,"* or *"my teacher is mean."* These thoughts can keep you from learning from authority, and can slow down your spiritual and intellectual growth. Furthermore, with the wrong thoughts, we may commit the same sin again.

Read
Apply
Obey
Pray

Bearing in mind that these unhealthy thoughts seem to be the easiest thoughts to have, we need to **make a habit** of giving thanks soon after we experience the setback.

Let us use Joseph as an example. He was punished and thrown in prison for something he never did. However, he didn't pout, or cry, or start a fight, or feel sorry for himself, or grow angry with God, or plan to retaliate, or get even. Joseph just continued to *please God.*

We please God when we overcome our setbacks *by being thankful for them.* The Holy Spirit will guide you:

Dear Heavenly Father,
I got punished, and I thank you for the authority in my life.
Amen.

If there is something in your life that you struggle to find how good can come from it, and are finding it hard to be thankful for how God may use this time for good, do these three things:

1. *pray* to God about it, and ask Him to reveal its good;

2. *read* your Bible and soak in the words you read; and

3. *talk* about it to a spiritual leader in your life, perhaps your mom or dad, or a church leader.

· · · · ·

Apply & Obey
by Chris

Bad days are going to happen. Because of the choices of Adam and his lovely wife Eve, bad days will always be a part of our life.

Looking at Joseph's life, one could say that *bad* days were a major part of his life experience. Little did Joseph know that a conversation with his brothers would start a "tidal wave" of bad days, leading him from a dark and dingy pit to being a slave and prisoner under Egyptian rule.

But God leads us, through His Word, to see that Joseph faced his bad days fearlessly. **Self-pity** was not a part of Joseph's DNA, nor should it be ours.

You see, although bad days are going to happen, feeling sorry for ourselves will only make bad days into terrible days. Normally our first response to having a bad day is "why me!?" Why are all these bad things happening today!?

God may be *giving* us that bad day to challenge us, and see whether we act in the flesh with *self-pity*, or do what Joseph did and keep our eyes on Him even on the toughest of days?

Two great scriptures to keep in mind when you have your next bad day (and yes, you will have them!) are **Ecclesiastes 7:14:**

In the day of prosperity be joyful, But in the day of adversity consider: Surely God has appointed the one as well as the other, So that man can find out nothing that will come after him.

and **James 1:2-5**:

My brethren, count it all joy when you fall into various trials, knowing that the testing of your faith produces patience. But let patience have its perfect work, that you may be perfect and complete, lacking nothing. If any of you lacks wisdom, let him ask of God, who gives to all liberally and without reproach, and it will be given to him.

Memorize these verses. You will need them, and they are a gift from our loving God. Add both verses to your memory verses list.

Dear Heavenly Father,
Thank You for always being near us.
No matter how bad some days get,
I thank You for Your will
and Your great plan.
Amen.

Lesson 4:

The "Presents" of God

Read (again) *Genesis 39:21.*

See in this verse that there are **three** blessings God gives to Joseph when Joseph was thrown into prison:
1. God was with Joseph;
2. God gave Joseph mercy; and
3. God gave Joseph favor in the sight of the keeper of the prison.

In verse 21, God gives us so much information, not just about Joseph, but about Himself. God wants you to take time to get to know **Him**. In Psalm 46:10, God commands, "Be still and know that I am God." Hence, let us obey.

First of all, God gives us His ***presence.***
Many verses up to this point state that "the LORD was with Joseph." Well, that's great. It is nice to know that God was with Joseph. However, considering God is everywhere and is aware of all that happens on His creation, not to mention that the statement "the LORD was with Joseph" has now been repeated at least three times in most Bible translations, you may think this part of the verse is a no-brainer. ***Why, then, would God include this exact same statement in the Bible more than once?***

One reason is because you and I are weak, and we constantly seem to forget that God is with us. If we did not forget that God is with us, we would never worry or be afraid.

Having bodyguards with us would surely keep us feeling courageous. They would always have our backs, and no one would try to come against us. No worries!

If a strong bodyguard can help us feel more courageous, how then can we be afraid when the Almighty God our Creator is with us, actually *with us?*

We become afraid for two reasons: *#1*, we do not know how great God is, and *#2*, we forget. Therefore, God has to remind us so many times that He is with us. Kind of sad, I know. That is why we need a Savior.

Apply and Obey

Look up the word Emmanuel and write the definition:

Emmanuel:

_____

_____

Now, look up **Leviticus 26:12**, and copy the verse in the space below:

_____

_____

_____

Memorize the verse, and add the verse to your memory verses list.

Dear Heavenly Father,
Thank You again for always being
near us. Help me to have courage and
faith in Your everlasting
presence.
Amen.

• • • • •

Apply & Obey

The second blessing that God wants you to see that He gives Joseph is **mercy.**

Mercy typically means to forgive someone for any wrong they have done, and to not give them the punishment they deserve. However, Joseph had done no wrong, so why would he need God's mercy?

Many Bible translations do not have the word *mercy* in verse 21, but the words *kindness* or *love*. The Book of Genesis was written by Moses in the Hebrew language. *Mercy* in ancient Hebrew translates to *loving kindness*. God wants you to see that He gave Joseph loving kindness.

Your life as a growing Christian man will be fruitful if you can remember that God wants to show you His incomparable love and kindness always and absolutely forever.

Look up **Jeremiah 31:3**, and write the verse in the space below:

_____

_____

_____

_____

Memorize this very popular verse, and add it to your memory verses list.

Dear Heavenly Father,
Thank You for salvation
through Jesus Christ. Thank You
for guiding me as Your own child.
I love You.
Amen.

•　•　•　•　•

Apply & Obey

The third blessing that God wants you to see that He gives Joseph is *favor.*

How nice it would be to always have God's favor in our lives! It seems then we would never fail, and never have bad days, but that is not what is meant by receiving God's favor.

The Bible says Joseph received God's favor, but that does not mean  Joseph always got what he wanted. It is very possible that Joseph still had to clean walls, sweep floors, and wash the feet of prison guards. He may have gone to sleep cold and hungry.

However, as he endured being a prisoner, a song of God's hope remained in his heart. He took on all tasks with peace in his eyes and with wisdom in his words. In all that he went through, the joy of the LORD remained his strength. This turned the heads of the leaders, and Joseph was well-respected.

When we are treated wrongly or put in an unfair situation, sometimes it seems that the best thing to do is to seek revenge, and to inform everyone as rudely as possible that we are red-hot mad.

However, here is when God shouts to you, "I love you! Just watch, listen, and see!" Here is where His love is stronger than whatever else is going on, and we can face the difficult unfair times in peace, reflecting God, and confidence in His powerful presence. God knows what is going on; He has it under control; He wants to give you this favor!

Look up **James 1:19,** and write it in the space below:

_____

_____

_____

Memorize the verse, and add the verse to your memory verses list.

As God's child, you have His presence, His mercy, and His favor. God wants you to know this, because He loves you!

You are loved by God way beyond your own measurement!

Dear Heavenly Father,
Thank You for Your favor upon us.
May I always be grateful just
Knowing You love me.
Amen.

Chapter 5
Seize the Day!
Genesis 40

"Carpe Diem" is Latin for "Seize the Day!" The words were actually written in a poem called "Odes" by a poet named Horace in 23 BC.

The words "Seize the Day" have remained strong words today and are even advice given to others. The words advise us to take the day fully, no matter what else is going on around you, and make the day matter for good! Live like you just know that this one day has a purpose in your life like no other day can.

If you do not live life to the fullest today, then when? Today is the day the LORD has made. Take what you have right now -- bruises, stinky socks, and all -- and make it beautiful. Make *this* day a day to remember. Please do not make it worth forgetting!

Whatever your hand finds to do, do it with all your might.
Ecclesiastes 9:10

Lesson 1:

A Baker & Butler's Dreams

Read *Genesis 40:1-23.*

Explanations in your reading:

The Baker and the Butler

These were two men that worked, were employed, with the Egyptian government, and had direct contact with the Pharaoh. Part of the butler's job was to serve Pharaoh his drink, but ONLY after the butler himself tested the drink by taking a sip to make sure the drink had not been poisoned. So, if the butler took a sip, tasted nothing funny, and lived, the Pharaoh could drink it. If the butler took a sip, tasted something strange in the drink, then fell over dead, then well, Pharaoh would not drink it. Yikes, scary job!

Why were they thrown in prison? The Bible does not say, but here is the scenario that I picture:

The Pharaoh becomes sick with terrible stomach pains. He is convinced that the sickness is from the food that the baker cooked for him and that the butler served him. "How dare they!" exclaims the Pharaoh, and he orders that they both be thrown in jail.

This is not in the Bible. It is just one possible explanation as to why the baker and the butler were thrown in jail.

Write your own thoughts and a summary of the reading:

_____

_____

_____

Dreams

The butler's dream was so hard for the butler to understand. Then he realizes that the baker, too, had a strange dream that same night. Confused, they agree that this is to be taken seriously. However, they do not know what to do. Their dreams seem impossible to understand. The dreams were part of God's plan. Joseph was going to have to completely trust God and submit to all that God showed him. Joseph was blessed by God with many things. One blessing was the gift to interpret dreams.

We still have dreams today. Some are fun and happy, some are scary, some are bizarre, and most are just plain crazy. So, how should we interpret our dreams today? *Should* we interpret our dreams? Do they have any meaning?

First of all, remember the importance and power of the Bible. There is no new discovery that is not already given to you by God that is not already written in the Bible. If I am pondering over my dreams more than I am pondering over God's words in the Bible, I will not get any worthy understanding. The Holy Word of God, prayer, and worship is to be our guide as we walk through life, not and never our dreams. Therefore, do not focus too much on them.

The study of dreams has been going on for centuries. The overall conclusion of dreams from a Christian standpoint is that most dreams are meaningless.

It shall be as when a hungry man dreams,
And look—he eats;
But he awakes, and his soul is still empty
...indeed he is faint,
And his soul still craves.
Isaiah 29:8

Can God still use dreams today? Absolutely, perhaps in His love for us. However, if we have easy access to His Word, we have an overflowing amount of His love, His directions, and His will. In **Jeremiah 23**, God instructs us to meditate on His word, not our dreams.

Why did God use dreams long ago? Dreams were a common tool God used to speak, in the Old and New Testament. Many words of the Bible were not yet written, or were not easily available. Therefore, God spoke directly to many people. Speaking through dreams makes sense: the person is being still when sleeping, and not talking or drowning out God's voice; therefore, God is able to speak.

What about the bad or scary dreams? Bad dreams are a horrible and strange matter to deal with. Children your age and younger endure many strange dreams due to your growing knowledge of the world around you. Many times you may go to bed with so much information on your brain, from school or TV; or, you may go to bed with emotions like sadness or anger. This heavy load may affect what and how we dream.

Be careful with what you eat close to bedtime. Certain foods, particularly sugar, may create some bizarre or bad dreams.

Dear Heavenly Father,
Thank You for being
the Peace in our lives. May I always
hold dear in my life the holy, powerful words
of the Bible.
Amen.

Lesson 2:
Hangin' On

Read Genesis 40:20-23.

Write your own thoughts and a summary of the reading:

_____

_____

_____

. . . . .

Waiting is in God's plan. God's hands at work in your life *seem* as if His hands are not there at all. *Have faith dear brother, and be strong.* Besides, God never promised easy; because easy is boring, and God is not boring.

It is *how we respond* to difficult times: the vacation was cancelled, or my sister breaks my bike, or it starts raining at the pool, or I've lost all my money, or I trip and fall in front of 100 people.

It is in these moments that GOD can strengthen us, and prepare us for His perfect plan! *Have faith!* Joseph gives the perfect example of faith, particularly in his honesty to the baker and the butler. He trusted God. Joseph had FAITH in God!

Apply & Obey
by Chris

Undoubtedly, the chief baker was hoping that Joseph was wrong in his interpretation when in Genesis 40:19, Joseph reveals, "Within three days Pharaoh will lift off your head from you and hang you on a tree; and the birds will eat your flesh from you." Unfortunately for the baker, Joseph's interpretation was *"dead on!"*

Joseph placed priority on truth, not on hurting someone's feelings. Ultimately, telling the truth without hesitation opened the door to Joseph's rise to power in Egypt.

Telling the truth without hesitation, even if it means that we may offend someone in the short term, will in the long term serve as a strong foundation in Godly character and in building integrity. Others around us will see that we can be trusted, because we're honest.

Look up **Hebrews 10:23**, and write the verse down in the space below:

_____

_____

_____

Memorize, and add to your memory verses list.

Dear Heavenly Father,
Thank you for being our Shepherd.
May my faith grow strong
so that I can do YOUR will.
Amen.

Chapter 6
God's Plan Unfolding
Genesis 41

Have you ever been told you were going through a growth spurt? One day, Mom seems like a giant, and the next day you are looking down just to make eye contact with her! Possibly a bit exaggerated, but growth does seem to be in "fast-forward" sometimes!

We go through *spiritual* growth spurts, too. When God is ready to give you His own special "miracle growth," be ready for full speed ahead! As long as you obey Him, you enter into one of the most amazing adventures of your life!

In Chapter 41, Joseph experiences a spiritual growth spurt. The chapter is packed FULL with insights into God's plan, and guidance for your *own* spiritual journey.

Lesson 1:
Check Me Out!

Read *Genesis 41:1-16.*

Write a summary and your own thoughts of the reading:

_____

_____

_____

· · · · ·

Joseph was seventeen years old when he was sold into slavery by his brothers, and taken to Egypt to work under Potiphar. He remained Potiphar's servant for approximately eleven years, and was then thrown into prison for at least two years. That's THIRTEEN YEARS that Joseph kept his faith and patience and waited upon the LORD! (A timeline of Joseph's life is in the appendix.)

And now, the Pharaoh himself seeks help from Joseph. This was a BIG deal – the Bible even informs us that Joseph put on clean clothes and shaved. A complete transformation! A chance for him to *really* get noticed and shine!....yet, Joseph gives all credit to God.

Apply & Obey
by Chris

Leadership without God fails every time. From a young age, Joseph knew that God was calling him into a leadership position. Although he had no clue as to what that position in leadership would entail, he faithfully chose to follow God's lead to get there.

Joseph would endure circumstances beyond his control, and far worse than what any of us will probably ever experience. Nonetheless, he stayed on course, keeping his focus on the Lord at all times.

As I reflect on God-led leadership and how it has impacted my own decisions as a leader, I am reminded of a note a former co-worker left with me before I embarked on my personal leadership journey. In the note, the former colleague wrote these words,

The "higher" you climb in your profession it seems

the less time you have to be with God.

Great men know that the higher you climb,

you have to be with God more, not less;

listen to Him more, and talk less;

and seek wise counsel more, not less.

I have held them close to my heart because of the profoundness and direction in which they point me on a daily basis. John 3:30 clearly states, "He must increase, but I must decrease." Let God lead you, not only in leadership, but in all aspects of life.

All that we have, all that we are, and all that we can do is from God. Read each verse below carefully. Then, choose two verses to memorize. Write the verses in the space below, and add the verses to your memory verses list. The verses below are from the New King James version. You may choose to use the version of your own Bible.

For of Him and through Him and to Him are all things, to whom be glory forever. Amen. Romans 11:36

"Let not the wise man glory in his wisdom,
Let not the mighty man glory in his might,
Nor let the rich man glory in his riches;
But let him who glories glory in this,
That he understands and knows Me,
That I am the LORD, exercising lovingkindness,
judgment, and righteousness in the earth.
For in these I delight," says the LORD.
Jeremiah 9:23,24

For by grace you have been saved through faith, and that
not of yourselves; it is the gift of God, not of works, lest
anyone should boast. Ephesians 2:8,9

I can do all things through Christ who strengthens me.
Philippians 4:13

But God forbid that I should boast except in the cross of
our Lord Jesus Christ.
Galatians 6:14

Verse #1:

_____
_____
_____
_____
_____

Verse #2:

_____

_____

_____

_____

_____

_____

_____

_____

Dear Heavenly Father,
Thank You for being our Provider.
May our boasting not be in ourselves,
but in You.
Amen.

Lesson 2:
The Bible

Read *Genesis 41:17-32.*

Write a summary and your own thoughts of the reading:

_____

_____

_____

• • • • •

The Pharaoh once again gives an account of his creepy, strange dream – cows eating cows. Oh, dear brother, I hope your stomach does not start twisting and turning on this one, because we are really going to dig deep into those cows!

This passage pours out an abundance of information. So much, that you may have forgotten many of the details, or just not understood it.

Read

Apply

Obey

Pray

There are many passages throughout the entire Bible that give loads of information, loads of spiritual insight, or loads of conviction on your own heart. *Take the time to take it all in.* There is no reason to rush through reading the Bible.

Here are some helpful ways to get the most out of your Bible reading:

1. **Pray** first. Ask for the Holy Spirit's guidance.
2. **Underline, highlight,** or **circle** words as you read to help you understand and remember more.

3. **Write** a summary of what you've read and how it spoke to you after you have finished reading, either in your Bible, or in a journal. In this Bible study, space is provided.

4. **Draw** pictures to make sense out of it, or to get a visual.

5. Refer to the **maps** in the back of your Bible to help you understand where all these things are taking place. A map is in the appendix of this book, but start using the maps in your own Bible as well.

What a wealth of knowledge and understanding you will have after going through these five steps. These are also good study tools for any school lesson you may have that requires challenging reading.

Apply & Obey

We are going to apply these five steps to **Genesis 17:32**. Complete steps one through three on your own, and then step 4 here. Therefore, on the following page entitled "Pharaoh's Dream," draw the following in order:

1. The Pharaoh standing by a river.

2. Seven skinny cows each with a fat cow in its mouth.

Do not worry about artistic quality. After all, you *are* drawing cows eating cows. I doubt it is a picture you would want to hang on your wall.

Pharaoh's Dream

(Standing by a river watching cow eat cows)

The next dream picture (weak stalk eating healthy stalk) is provided for you:

Now hopefully, you have a better understanding of Pharaoh's God-given dream.

Making your own visual of the Bible reading gives a better understanding of what is going on. Try the steps above anytime you are reading the Bible and get stumped.

Now that it makes better sense, we will move deeper into God's Word.

Dear Heavenly Father,
Thank you for being our Guide
in the days You alone have given us.
May we take the time to understand
all the words You have provided for us
in the Bible.
Amen.

Lesson 3:

Can I See What You See?...

Read *Genesis 41:33-45.*

Explanations in your reading:

v. 34   "...produce of the land..." Produce, such as corn, wheat, vegetables, fruit, tree nuts, and tree fruit were planted after the Nile flooded, and then harvested once per year.

v. 42   "...took his signet ring off..." The word *"signet"* means a seal, or sealed (It is where we get the word *"sign."*) There was a seal or an engraving on Pharaoh's ring that was a symbol of his authority over Egypt. The ring could also work as a stamp on documents approved by the Pharaoh. Joseph now has the authority to approve or disapprove any issues in Egypt. That is a whole lot of trust!

v. 45   "...Zaphnath-Paaneah..." The name may mean "He Speaks," or "Life Giver."

v.45   "...On..." An Egyptian city. (See map in Appendix.)

Write a summary and your own thoughts of the reading:

_____

_____

_____

· · · · ·

The Pharaoh was given news that the rest of the world did not know, a famine was coming. Not only was Joseph able to interpret the Pharaoh's dreams, but Joseph also courageously offered the Pharaoh a wise plan to avoid starving during the famine. Pharaoh is impressed, and Joseph is rewarded: he is given the Pharaoh's signet ring, royal clothes, a gold chain, a new name, a new wife, power and authority, a chariot, and even a parade!

No verses speak of Joseph's feelings or emotions up to this point. We know of nothing that troubles his mind, or of what may make him sad. However, we can see his **thoughts** through his **actions** and his **words**.

Our thoughts are shown through our actions and through our words.

For example, we can tell that a volcano is about to erupt by what is

happening on the *outside* …animals and birds behave differently and flee the area, nearby streams and creeks may dry up, the mountain that surrounds the volcano becomes bigger. Hence, there is no doubt what is happening *inside* that volcano.

We can also tell it is going to rain soon by looking at the sky. The sun is

covered in thick clouds. The wind begins to blow. There is no doubt of what is *inside* those clouds.

People **noticed** that Joseph, a slave, obeyed and respected Potiphar. The prison keeper **noticed** Joseph's strong work ethic, and trustworthiness.

Potipher's wife **heard** Joseph refuse to sin against God. The baker and the butler **heard** Joseph give all credit of dreams to God. The Pharaoh **heard** Joseph's words, "It is not me, but God…"

So, we do not see any feelings or emotions that Joseph may have been having during this time, but we do see his actions, and we hear his words. Therefore, we have a pretty good idea of Joseph's thoughts. His thoughts were to please God.

Joseph had integrity, as we studied in Chapter 4. Our thoughts, oftentimes, need to be kept in check.

Apply & Obey

To practice keeping the joy of the Lord in our thoughts, write down how you can remember and think of God with each thing. I will do the first one.

Donuts: *They have no ending or beginning, like God!*

Sunshine: _____

Shoes: _____

Snow: _____

Friends: _____

Chores: _____

I wish I could see *your* answers!

The point of this exercise is to see how we need to keep our focus on God, and this will pour out into our words and into our actions.

Here are two amazing verses to hide deep in your heart *(and in your thoughts!)*...

Look up **Philippians 3:8**, and copy it in the space below:

_____

_____

_____

_____

_____

Now look up and copy **Mark 12:30** in the space below:

_____

_____

_____

_____

Memorize these verses, and add them to your memory verses list.

Dear Heavenly Father,
Thank You for being so merciful as
we try to grow closer to You. Show us
our hearts, O Lord, and lead us into the
way of everlasting.
Amen.

Lesson 4:
Trust Me

Read *Genesis 41:46-52.*

Write a summary and your own thoughts of the reading:

_____

_____

_____

.   .   .   .   .

Joseph was *dependable*, or trusted, or one that others came to for help. If *we* are dependable, we are known for meeting the needs of others.

Apply & Obey

The practice of dependability in your life starts at *home*.

We are going beyond obedience here. All be it, obedience *is* crucial. Dependability largely leaps further, and it is practiced by just helping others – being a servant.

To suit up as a dependable man of God, like Joseph, you need **THREE** main essentials: *love, wisdom,* and *self-denial*. Focus on each of these whole-heartedly and carefully.

1. LOVE: When we love others, we want to help them and be there for them.

1 John 3:16-18 NIV

This is how we know what love is: Jesus Christ laid down
His life for us. And we ought to lay down our lives for
our brothers. If anyone has material possessions and
sees his brother in need but has no pity on him, how can
the love of God be in him? Dear children, let us not love
with words or tongue but with actions and in truth.

**Write a summary and your own thoughts of this scripture in
regards to how you can be dependable through LOVE:**

_____

_____

_____

Potiphar, the jail-keeper, and Pharaoh knew that Joseph loved them;
therefore, Joseph was trusted. Underline or highlight these verses in
your Bible, and add them to your memory verses list.

Dear Heavenly Father,
Thank You for being LOVE,
and for Your Bible as we are guided
to be dependable.
Amen.

•   •   •   •   •

2. WISDOM: Pray for wisdom, dear brother; God will

give it liberally. With wisdom, we learn in life to have the courage and
the drive to make the right choices. Through wisdom, we learn that life
is worthy when we try to please God.

Therefore, we spend our time *wisely*, we spend our money *wisely*, we make *wise* decisions, and others know they can depend on us when we reflect our wisdom.

Growing wisdom starts by reading your Bible. These following verses reflect God as your Dad, telling you how to behave yourself *(in the loving way that only GOD can do!)*:

Psalm 1:1-3 NKJV

Blessed is the man who walks not in the counsel of the ungodly,

nor stands in the path of sinners,

nor sits in the seat of the scornful;

(v.2) But his delight is in the law of the LORD, and in His law he meditates day and night.

(v.1) He shall be like a tree planted by the rivers of water, that brings forth its fruit in its season, whose leaf also shall not wither; and whatever he does shall prosper.

Write a summary and your own thoughts of this scripture in regards to being dependable through WISDOM:

_____

_____

_____

Joseph conveyed wisdom, and was therefore trusted with all that other leaders possessed.

*Dear Heavenly Father,
Thank You for being my
Dad. You show me how to live
every day so I can have wisdom.
Amen.*

• • • • •

3. Self-Denial: We need to deny ourselves in order to

be dependable. Self-denial is forgetting what is fair, forgetting my own wants, desires, and needs, and thanking God for the opportunity to give to someone else.

Philippians 2:3,4
Let nothing be done through selfish ambition or conceit, but in lowliness of mind let each esteem others better than himself. Let each of you look out not only for his own interests, but also for the interests of others. Let this mind be in you which was also in Christ Jesus.

Write a summary and your own thoughts of this scripture in regards to being dependable through SELF-DENIAL:

_____

_____

_____

To *practice* denying yourself, start encouraging others more. Cheer for your siblings. Compliment Mom and Dad. Encourage anyone who needs encouragement.

Then, you will find that your focus in life is no longer on just you, but on others. Have you heard this acrostic before?...

Jesus

Others

You!

The addends that sum up dependability in our own lives are

Love + Wisdom + Self-Denial = Dependability.

These were attributes of Joseph; therefore, all of the world depended on Joseph to feed their families and keep them living!

Dear Heavenly Father,
Thank You for being Wonderful,
and for helping me to become a
dependable young man. May I always
hunger for Your Word as I grow.
Amen.

Lesson 5:

REAP!

(...but sow first!)

Read *Genesis 41:53-57.*

Explanations in your reading:

v. 51, "Manasseh" and "Ephraim." How Joseph named his
52 children reflects what was in his heart: Manasseh reminds Joseph that God heals every hurt, so he can let go of bad memories. Ephraim reminds Joseph to praise God for his blessings. Powerful names!

Write a summary and your own thoughts of the reading:

_____

_____

_____

• • • • •

To clarify what is going on, we will briefly focus on harvesting and farming. You may have already learned in a history class at school some interesting facts about the Nile River that runs through Egypt. Farming depended on the Nile River. Every year, the Nile would flood the farmlands, which was a good thing, because the flood primed the farmland land with rich soil.

Hence, wheat and other crops were planted after the flood, and then harvested once per year before the next flood came. The wheat, or grain, was stored in granaries (storerooms, barns) or silos. Considering they also lived on the Nile, fish was a major source of food. The Egyptians may have canned their fish and other meats. Egypt was also blessed with tree fruit and tree nuts. The Egyptians had great soil, great food, and an abundant life of plenty – more than plenty. They may have lived as if they could afford to waste food. They may have thrown piles of leftover food in the trash, thinking nothing of it.

Imagine that you and your family have been told that all grocery stores are completely EMPTY! The food that you have in your house is all you will have for *seven months*. How would things in your family change? What would each family member need to do to see that you and your family would not starve? Ask your family for help, and list some ideas here:

_____

_____

_____

_____

_____

Some of your ideas are probably good practices to follow even as the grocery stores remain open and full of food for sale. Are there any ideas above that you believe may be good for you and your family to follow today and every day? Is so, why?

_____

_____

_____

The wise have wealth and luxury, but fools spend whatever they get.
Proverbs 21:20

Apply & Obey
by Chris

We have turned into a "just-can't-wait" society, where anything we could possibly want is only a click of a button away. This can be handy, but can also feed our selfish desire for *instant gratification.*

In Genesis 37:9, the Bible says, "Then he dreamed another dream and told it to his brothers, and said, "Look, I have dreamed another dream. And this time, the sun, the moon, and the eleven stars bowed down to me." Although he knew God was calling him for a special purpose, it would be many years until this calling came to complete fruition. But never once does the Bible say that Joseph complained about God's timing for his calling. Joseph trusted God's timing for his life and so should we.

In **Romans 8:28**, the Bible promises,

> *"And we know that all things work together for good to those who love God, to those who are the called according to His purpose."*

I can imagine that Joseph had similar thoughts on his rise to greatness. Our selfish desires can be insatiably fed in this sinful world, *but only if we feed our desires!*

Look up **Proverbs 21:20**, and write the verse below:

_____

_____

_____

Memorize this verse, and add the verse to your memory verses list.

Dear Heavenly Father,
Thank you for being our
Provider. May we be wise with all
You give us, taking care of what we have,
and not spending or wasting
foolishly.
Amen.

Reflection of Jesus

Joseph was the ONE person in the *whole* world that people knew they could go to and be fed, and be given food for their family.

In Genesis 41:57, the Bible says "the famine was severe," meaning the people across the world were more than just hungry. Their crops were now just *dry ground*. Without food, they became *weak*, and many became *sick* and *died*. Far away from Egypt, families heard of a man in Egypt who had an abundance of food, and if they could just get to him, they knew their family would LIVE!

We seek Jesus the same way. He is the ONE person in the whole world that we can go to and be fed. The famine in our lives today is *sin*. This "famine" has plagued the *whole* world. Many try to fill their hunger with nice things, other gods, or self-indulgences and *more sin*. Consequently, they are NEVER filled. On the other hand, those who seek Jesus are always given salvation, all sins are washed away, and are given assurance of eternal LIFE!

And Jesus said to them, "I am the bread of life. He who comes to Me shall never hunger, and he who believes in Me shall never thirst." John 6:35

Reflection of YOU

We are to give nourishment to those that are starving. Be the hands and feet of Jesus, and be ready and willing to pray for someone, smile at someone, and help someone. Ask Jesus to fill *you*, and then be a friend, and share the love of Jesus Christ, so others can LIVE!

Chapter 7
Family
Genesis 42

"But what if...?" my own son would often ask before having a task to accomplish. For example, I request, "Please go ask the neighbor for a cup of sugar." A most common reply I received, "*What if* she's not home?...*What if* she doesn't have any sugar?...*What if* she gets mad?...*What if* she asks me to come inside?...*What if* I eat just a little of the sugar?..."

While it is driving me *crazy* and I am sure there MUST be a mute button somewhere on him, I think of my own "what if" questions: what if I never had these fun and funny moments with my children? What if I had no family to share my thoughts with? What if I did not have the family that God gave me?

Although our families may have friction, tension, or even serious problems, there are really no other people in all the *world* that touches our hearts like our family members.

In Genesis 42, we will go back home to Hebron with Jacob and all of Joseph's brothers, and see how hearts, maybe even your own, gets touched!

Lesson 1:

Spies?

Read *Genesis 42:1-14.*

Explanations in your reading:

v. 4 "…did not send Benjamin…" Remember, Benjamin was the youngest brother of the twelve, and the last son Rachel had before she died. Now that Joseph is dead (or so Jacob believes), Benjamin is the only part of Rachel that Jacob has left, and he does not want to lose him, too.

v. 8 Joseph's brothers did not recognize him. It has been 22 years since Joseph was sold into slavery. An age and time chart is located in the appendix. He has changed by growing, but he is also dressed as a very rich Egyptian, much more elaborate than a coat of many colors. Joseph is possibly even wearing make-up, which was part of the Egyptian culture during that time period.

v. 9 "You are spies…" Explanation on the next page.

Write a summary and your own thoughts of the reading:

_____

_____

_____

· · · · ·

Egypt became a popular place. Joseph now sits on the throne as governor. He has made a name for himself as one of the most popular men in the world. He is known as "Zaphnath-Paaneah."
The word even spread to Hebron.

Why did Joseph call his brothers spies? Is he trying to get revenge?

Joseph knew they were not spies. Think of how the brothers looked: ten foreigners (the brothers) traveling a long distance down to Egypt, claiming they were all brothers that needed food... it looked suspicious. It looked so suspicious that these men are brought before the highly honored Egyptian Governor. Little did these ten men know that this great power of a man was their nagging little brother Joseph!

Although Joseph knew these men were his brothers, he had a job to do. Joseph was expected to question these ten strange foreigners. Not to mention, these brothers of Joseph did not exactly have a reputation of being honest, kind, and loving. How did Joseph not know if the brothers came to fight and take all that Egypt had? Joseph's job was to protect Egypt, and he knew these men had the capability of being bad guys.

We can only imagine those first few seconds: when Joseph saw his brothers, do you think his eyes got big, or maybe his chin dropped? Or do you think he gasped when he saw them, or became nervous?

Benjamin was not with the brothers, and perhaps the only way Joseph would ever see Benjamin again was to put some fear in the brothers.

You may be thinking, "Joseph was being mean to his brothers," or "Joseph is getting them back and giving his mean brothers what they deserve." These thoughts did cross *my* mind, too; but something didn't seem right.

Joseph is a man of the one true God in the midst of Egyptian fake gods. That had to be a very powerful relationship between Joseph and God. Therefore, I think Joseph did not feel like he had to get revenge on his brothers. Joseph remembered the dreams from God and knew God was in control. So, there would have been no need for Joseph to seek vengeance.

Apply & Obey

Vengeance is not godly. Vengeance is carried out when we're angry, fed up with, or insulted, and we lose faith in God and decide to take matters into our own hands. Vengeance is carried out usually within a split second and really reveals the heart. Vengeance never has good consequences, and it leaves us angry still!

Self-control will help us remember that God loves the person that has upset us.

Love covers a multitude of sins.
1 Peter 4:8

Look up and read **1 Peter 4:8-9** in your Bible. Write the 8th verse in the space below:

_____

_____

_____

Memorize the verse, and add the verse to your memory verses list.

Dear Heavenly Father,
Thank You for being All-Powerful.
Shower us with self-control, and guide us
to love one another and to be hospitable
to one another.
Amen.

Lesson 2:
The Good Fear

Read *Genesis 42:15-24.*

Explanations in your reading:

v. 21   The brothers are speaking to one another in Hebrew, thinking Joseph does not understand what they are saying. The brothers believe their sin against Joseph 22 years ago is now being paid. They are also revealing to us that they have held on to this guilt for 22 years!

v. 22   Reuben is basically saying, "I told you so!" Joseph now learns that Reuben had nothing to do with it.

v. 23   Joseph has learned the Egyptian language and culture in the years he has spent in Egypt. He is now bilingual, knowing the Egyptian language and his home language, Hebrew. So when his brothers speak to one another, they do not know that Joseph understands them. Also, Joseph must be speaking to his brothers in the Egyptian language, because an interpreter was present.

v. 24   All the feelings of being thrown away like trash by his brothers return. These feelings resurface. This is the first time we actually see extreme emotion in Joseph.

Write a summary and your own thoughts of the reading:

_____

_____

_____

· · · · ·

Benjamin, Joseph's only full-blooded brother (meaning they have the same mother and father), is not among the brood of brothers being questioned by Joseph, and Joseph misses Benjamin terribly.

Joseph enlightens the brothers in verse 18, noting that he "fears God." He was informing them that he knows what pleases and displeases God, and that he chooses to NOT sin against God.
Have you noticed that every time Joseph speaks, he refers to **God**?
What does it mean to "fear God?" Fearing God is knowing that God is HOLY, PERFECT, and JUST, and that the most *dreadfulness* we can ever have in our lives is sinning, because it takes us away from God; and because God is perfect, we will face the consequences of our sin – *never* fun, and *never* worth it.

Therefore, as God's children, we fear God, because we always want to stay close to God.

Apply & Obey

Read all three verses, and copy the *last* verse (Proverbs 1:7) and memorize:

And the LORD commanded us to observe all these statutes, to fear the LORD our God, for our good always, that he might preserve us alive, as it is this day. Deuteronomy 6:24

Oh, how great is Your goodness, Which you laid up for those who fear You. Which You have prepared for those who trust in You in the presence of the sons of men! Psalm 31:19

The fear of the LORD is the beginning of knowledge, but fools despise wisdom and instruction. Proverbs 1:7

Dear Heavenly Father,
Thank You for being our perfect, holy,
and faithful God! May we fear You because
we know that You love us, and because
we love You.
Amen.

Reflection of Jesus

Temptations

Both Jesus and Joseph remained *steadfast* and *immovable*, although they lived around the worship of false gods. Jesus never sinned and He shared the love of God. Joseph, as the youngest brother, did not partake in his brother's sins, and he remained righteous while in prison; and faithful and honest throughout the temptations of Potiphar's wife. Yet, worldly, wicked choices were around them all the time. It seems the temptations around them would have made them "bend."

Therefore, my brethren, be steadfast, immovable, always abounding in the work of the Lord, knowing that your labor is not in vain in the Lord. 1 Corinthians 15:58

Reflection of YOU

How can we, like Jesus, remain faithful and righteous to God in times of temptation? The Bible commands us to be steadfast and immovable.

Steadfast means "to be firm and unwavering." Immovable means, of course, "cannot be moved." To be as such, keep a close relationship with God, pray to Him and talk to Him throughout the day. Sin can be enticing, but don't move! Stay firm, unwavering, and unmoved!

Pray and ask God to help you stay steadfast and immovable to overcome the temptations of sin.

Lesson 3:
What a Burden

Read *Genesis 42:25-38.*

Explanations in your reading:

v. 25 "...restore every man's money..." Joseph gave the brothers food to take home for free; the money they used to pay for their food was placed back with all they had.

v. 27 Apparently, Joseph replaced the money without the brothers knowing, leaving the brothers to think they did not pay for the food they took out of Egypt.

v. 28 "What is this that God has done to us?" Interesting. The fear of God is *finally* getting into their hearts. They are feeling uneasy because it looks as if they stole the money.

v. 36 Jacob may have thought Simeon was killed in Egypt.

v. 37 "Kill my two sons..." Is this realistic? Does Reuben really expect Jacob to kill his own grandsons? Jacob is not moved by Reuben's offer.

Write a summary and your own thoughts of the reading:

_____

_____

_____

• • • • •

After the turmoil the brothers had in Egypt, they all returned home to their father and reported the bad news, honestly this time.

Over the past 13 or so years, the brothers and their father Jacob have remained a close family. None of the brothers left (too far away) to live in a foreign land, none have died, and none of them seem to be angry with another. It appears that, until now, the family of Jacob (or Israel) has lived in peace and in harmony with one another, supposedly burying their lie.

Something Good about the Brothers...

So far, the brothers have been the "bad guys" through the life of Joseph. However, now they are willing to do whatever they need to do to make their father happy. In chapter 42, the brothers have shown *guilt* for mistreating Joseph, *respect* for Egyptian authority, and they have shown *reverence* for their own father. They are reflecting *perseverance* as they work together as *a team* to find a solution. Here are the burdens on their shoulders:

- They sold their own brother into slavery.
- They lied to their father about Joseph being dead, and never told him the truth.
- Their families are going hungry because of the famine.
- They are treated roughly by Egyptian authority.
- They are forced to leave a brother in Egyptian prison (Simeon).
- They fear the Egyptian government will arrest them for stealing food.
- They see that their own father is in great despair.
- They have to hurt their father even more by taking Benjamin to Egypt.

"There is no peace," says my God, "for the wicked."
Isaiah 57:21

Write the above verse down, memorize, and add it to your memory verses list.

_____

_____

_____

Sin causes suffering. Through that suffering, we can choose to pout in anger foolishly, or *humbly accept* the punishment and grow closer to God. The brothers of Joseph are accepting humility.

Dear Heavenly Father,
Thank You for being our Provider
of Righteousness. Show us our hearts
and see if there is a wicked or offensive way
in us, and lead us to be with YOU forever.
Amen.

Chapter 8
Fellowship
Genesis 43

No one has to be a "social butterfly" to fellowship. You do not have to have a huge group of friends, you do not have to be popular, and you do not necessarily have to know anyone in the group.

Having fellowship with others is an adventure; not on the same level as, perhaps, a roller coaster or a tropical vacation. Nonetheless, if you really take part in fellowship with others, you see so many different, unique paths that each person is walking with God. One person is rejoicing over an accomplishment, while another is grieving or looking for hope.

In fellowship, you have the opportunity to share your own heart with others, to listen as others share, to make a new friend, to help someone out, to laugh and have fun, and to praise God together. This is a huge opportunity for God to work in your life, and you have the chance to see God working in someone else's life.

Unlike roller coasters and tropical vacations, fellowship is an adventure that can changed the rest of your life!

Lesson 1:
Maybe Later

Read Genesis 43:1-14.

Write a summary and your own thoughts of the reading:

_____

_____

_____

• • • • •

This part of Genesis 43 is fun to read. It is mostly dialogue, and it is interesting to see how the family speaks to each other.

Verse 2 states, *And it came to pass, when they had eaten up the grain which they had brought from Egypt, that their father said to them, "Go back, buy us a little food."*

Apparently, after the heated discussion the family had at the end of chapter 42, no one wanted to talk about it. It was swept under the rug, although Brother Simeon sits in Egyptian jail waiting. It is not brought up again until they get hungry again. The brothers seemingly did not dare bring it up again. So Jacob did.

Apply & Obey

There are many things in our lives that we do not feel like taking care of right away, because it is too hard, or it is boring, or it will take too long, or because we just do not want to do it. Some examples may be cleaning out your closet, cleaning out from under your bed, doing your homework, practicing ball or music, apologizing to someone, helping someone out, spending time with family, or reading your Bible. The longer we take to complete what needs to be completed, the more it becomes a burden. It is called *procrastinating*.

Look up, read, and write **Psalm 119:60** below, and memorize the verse:

_____

_____

_____

Remember to add this verse to your memory verses list.

This is a great verse to say over and over and over again in your head and when you're faced with an unwanted task!

Dear Heavenly Father,
Thank You for being our Strength,
So that we can always make haste and
not delay to keep Your commandments.
Amen.

Lesson 2:
Dinner Party

Read *Genesis 43:15-34.*

Explanations in your reading:

v. 18   Joseph now lived in one of the wealthiest homes in Egypt.

v. 24   The steward of Joseph's home was very kind to the brothers, as ordered by Joseph. Do you think Joseph confided in the steward and told him that the men were his brothers that sold him as a slave? Or did the steward simply obey Joseph's commands without question?

v. 32   Egyptian custom was that Egyptians and Hebrews did not eat together. Although they were invited to dinner, they were not allowed to sit with Joseph (now considered an Egyptian) or any other Egyptians who may have been present.

v. 33   Joseph had the brothers sit in order of their age. In their head, the brothers are thinking, *"What* is going on?"

Write a summary and your own thoughts of the reading:

_____

_____

_____

• • • • •

Like Benjamin, have *you* ever had someone so excited to see you that they have to excuse themselves because they get choked up with tears? If not, no worries; neither have I.

This reminds me of a video I watched of a young child performing cheers on a football field. She looked to her left, and standing some yards away was her dad in his military uniform, staring and smiling at her. She was so surprised to see her father who, I am sure, had been serving overseas in the military. The little girl had such a priceless face of shock when she saw him, and she started running to her dad just as fast as she could run. Her dad picked her up, and as they hugged, she cried. I imagined how many days and nights she wondered if she would ever see her father again, and having to live each day accepting the fact that she very well may not. Yet on this day, God's grace shined brightly upon her.

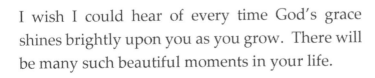

Joseph's feelings may have been similar to the little girl when he saw Benjamin. He was never sure he would see his little brother again. Yet, there Benjamin stood, looking back at Joseph. Joseph chose to continue to keep his identity hidden, and he kept his feelings for Benjamin in secret. God's grace shined brightly upon Joseph.

Read
Apply
Obey
Pray

I wish I could hear of every time God's grace shines brightly upon you as you grow. There will be many such beautiful moments in your life.

A loving verse of God's eternal grace is Jeremiah 31:3:

"Yes, I have loved you with an everlasting love; therefore with lovingkindness I have drawn you."
Jeremiah 31:3

You already have this verse in your list. Re-memorize this verse, and remember that God WANTS to pour His love and blessings on you, because God loves you so incredibly, immeasurably much!

Dear Heavenly Father,
Thank for being LOVE, and for loving us,
and gracing us with Your unmatchable love.
We love YOU, too!
Amen.

Chapter 9
The Valley of Death
Genesis 44

My pastor asked the congregation an interesting question one Sunday morning: "Can God bless a man greatly if he has not suffered deeply?" I then thought of Jacob's brothers.

The confrontation that the brothers had with Joseph may have possibly been the first time they stopped to think about the sin in their lives and feel any remorse. Up to this point, since selling their little brother, they may have thought there was no need to even think about pleasing God.

God loves a contrite heart. When we show God our broken heart, God can show us unimaginable blessings, like His power, His love, His guidance, His will, His blessings, and His mercy.

When I tearfully pour my heart out to God (not whining or complaining, but hurt, confused or sad), His love and glory floods into my heart. As a Christian, even in our weakest moments, the peace of God is there.

Psalm 34:18 explains, *"The LORD is near to those who have a broken heart, and saves such as have a contrite spirit."*

Lesson 1:

Where Do You Think You're Going?

Read Genesis 44:1-16.

Explanations in your reading:

v. 13 "they tore their clothes." This action is in the Bible quite a few times. It is an action of expressing great grief.

v. 15 "…can practice divination?" Divination is the ability to predict what is going on (who took the cup). Divination is evil in God's eyes, but was practiced in Egypt. Joseph, more than likely, was not serious with the brothers, although God did gift him as such.

v. 16 "God has found out…" Judah understands that God sees and has seen their sins. This is progress. He is paying more attention to all that matters – God.

v. 16 "…your servants…" A synonym for "us" or "me" or "we." It was a respectful way to communicate with others. For example, your servant is pleased that you are currently studying Joseph… I am calling myself "your servant," to show you that I honor you and will serve you.

Write a summary and your own thoughts of the reading:

_____

_____

_____

.　.　.　.　.

Can you imagine being one of Joseph's brothers in Egypt? Imagine you are a grown man, and one of the ten brothers of Joseph, taking another trip to Egypt. After a long, dusty travel from Hebron, you and your brothers are surprised that the authorities do not only give your brother Simeon back, but they prepare a nice meal in the house of royalty for all of you! Then, you and your brothers are given money and loads of food for free! You and your brothers are completely confused, but decide it was just a great night. Those Egyptians were so kind and hospitable! Although terribly strange, what a wonderful evening and nice dinner! You all leave together, relieved that no more tragedy has taken place. Eager to see satisfaction on your dad's (Jacob's) face, all the brothers head home.

Nonetheless, on your journey home, royal Egyptian authorities come charging toward you on their horses, and *once again*, you and your brothers are accused of being thieves!

The delightful evening has flipped into a nightmare!

What is going on? From the brothers' point of view, this is crazy! What is Joseph doing? Why does he not just say. "I'm Joseph! Now off with your heads!"

Nevertheless, before you take a side between Joseph or the brothers (and possibly judge one side or the other), try to look at the entire picture.

Suppose Joseph wrote a letter to his brothers to reveal his heart, and suppose you are one of the brothers receiving the letter. Let's read what Joseph has to say:

Dear Brothers,

Please take the time to understand how every moment in my own life has been constantly changing, with most of it in turmoil and confusion. Please take this time to see how I see, and to know me more. I felt that same despair that you are feeling right now. I have felt that same grief and confusion, wondering why horror follows me. Dark, frustrating thoughts filled my mind as well. I did right before God, like you. Then I was pushed down, enslaved, and imprisoned.

It hurts badly for me to look at my brother Benjamin's face, and see my own mother; yet, he does not even know me. He thinks I am dead, nonexistent.

I have wondered every day if I would ever see my loving father again. For so many years, I wondered if I would ever see a day of freedom again. It's such a horrible feeling.

I know, and now you know.

I don't want to see you suffer, but through this time may you reflect on me, and come to know me. Perhaps now our hearts are becoming closer together. I want you to know me. For this moment, be like me. Then you will know me and understand me, and hopefully, you will love me.

Love,
Joseph

Reflection of Jesus
Seeing Truth

Jesus came to live among us. Like Joseph with his brothers, Jesus **longs to be closer to us.** Jesus wants us to completely **know Him,** because He loves us.

Many viewed Jesus as a trouble-maker, but He is the Prince of Peace:
"For the Son of Man did not come to destroy men's lives but to save them." Luke 9:56

Jesus explained the story of "The Prodigal Son" in Luke 15:11-32. The parable involves two sons that take different paths. One son is greedy and sinful, and for a long time, he is blind to his sin. The other son is devoted and obedient, living with their father. It is only until the greedy son opens his eyes that he runs into his father's arms, repenting. His father is grateful that the son opened his eyes to *the truth,* and then knew to *seek truth and love.*

Jesus exclaims:
"And you shall know the truth, and the truth shall make you free."
John 8:32

Joseph knew the torment of not seeing truth kept his brothers from seeing who he really was.

Reflection of You

What sin or weakness is trying to hide in your life, so that you won't know it is there? What temptation for sin may be growing stronger in your own life?

Challenge yourself to pray **Psalm 139:23,24** every day, and be prepared for God to answer:

"Search me,
O God, and know my heart;
Try me, and know my anxieties
See if there is a wicked way in me,
And lead me into the way
Of Everlasting.
Amen."

Lesson 2:
Liar, Liar!

Read *Genesis 44:17-34.*

Write a summary and your own thoughts of the reading:

_____

_____

_____

. . . . .

Judah

Considering there are so many brothers, it may seem difficult to keep up with which one's which.

Judah was the fourth oldest son. His mother was Leah. Even though Judah was not the oldest, he seemed to be a leader among the brothers. Judah is the brother that suggested to all the brothers that Joseph be sold. He was also the only brother that could convince their father Jacob to allow Benjamin to go back to Egypt with them. Judah is also a descendent of Jesus Christ – it is from Judah's lineage that Jesus was born!

I am sure you have noticed that the title of this lesson is "Liar, Liar!" But why? We have two men that have proclaimed two lies here: *#1*, Joseph claims that Benjamin stole his royal cup (although Joseph was trying to act out of love for his brothers by keeping them close to him, he did so dishonestly!), and *#2*, Judah claims that one brother is dead. That is a *lie!* Judah and his brothers do not know what happened to Joseph. They lied to their father about Joseph's death 22 years ago, and are *still* saying that

Joseph is dead. Judah has been lying for such a long time, it sounds like he may believe his own lie! This conversation between Judah and Joseph is intense.

Joseph lied either to keep his brothers close, or to see how they would react toward Benjamin. Judah lied to protect himself. Neither lie meant any harm; however, lies are always about me, me, and always me!

Apply & Obey

We know lying is wrong. One of our Ten Commandments states, "Do not bear false witness."

Lying is a poison. Once we start lying, this horrible brew of gunk simmers and boils in our lives: we lose trust from others, we cannot be depended upon, we stop maturing, and we stop learning about God and wisdom.

Choose at least one verse to write down in the space below and memorize. Remember, these verses are from the New King James Version. Use your own Bible translation, if you prefer:

Lying lips are an abomination to the LORD, but those who deal truthfully are His delight. Proverbs 12:22

Let no corrupt word proceed out of your mouth, but what is good, that he may have something to give him who has need. Ephesians 4:29

Do not lie to one another, since you have put off the old man with his deeds. Colossians 3:9

Let the words of my mouth and the meditation of my heart be acceptable in Your sight, O LORD, my strength and my Redeemer.
Psalm 19:14

_____

_____

_____

_____

Add the verses or verse to your memory verses list.

Dear Heavenly Father,
Thank You for being Truth.
May the words of my mouth and
the meditation of my heart be acceptable in
Your sight, O LORD, my strength
and my Redeemer.
Amen.

Chapter 10
Family
Genesis 45

Let's get gloomy and morbid for a moment. Imagine something tragic happens to you. You injure yourself, you become disabled, you fail miserably at something that meant the world to you, you lose someone you love, or maybe you come near death yourself. Feeling gloomy? Good.

Now imagine: who in this world is the most affected because of your tragedy, friends? neighbors? Hollywood? your school? your community? your church? *or your family?*

Your family is feeling hurt, anguished. *Your family* is rigorously praying for you. No one is hoping for you to be given an abundant life like *your family*. It is not that others do not care for you and love you, but family has a special seat in our lives that should **always** be held in high regard.

God gave you your particular family, with all the quirks and strange habits and embarrassment you can stand. All the same, this is where God's will for your life starts. This is where you practice love, joy, patience, peace, kindness, goodness, faithfulness, gentleness, and self-control.

Family is where you learn that God is love.

Lesson 1:
Brotherly Reunion

Read *Genesis 45:1-15.*

Explanations in your reading:

v. 10   Goshen – you will find on the map in the appendix.

v. 3, 4   "I am Joseph." He had to say it twice. How do you think the brothers responded the first time he said it? They may have thought, "What did he say?" or "Joseph? He has the same name as our brother!"

v. 6   "…there are five years of famine left…" The brothers are not aware of Joseph's prophecy of famine for 7 years. They have been hoping for rain every day. This is the first time they have heard that the famine will last another 5 whole years!

Write a summary and your own thoughts of the reading:

_____

_____

_____

· · · · ·

So much is on Joseph's mind right now: he sees God's complete control, he is finding forgiveness in his heart for the brothers, and he longs to share his heart with them. He misses his dad. All of this causes Joseph to *weep*.

Apply & Obey Part I

After all that has happened in Joseph life, he completely gives credit to God.

"God sent me here."

Precious brother, how much richer could our lives be if we daily said the same words, whether we are stuck with our mom at the grocery store, at school, or visiting Grandma.

"God sent me here."

Write these same words down on a small piece of paper, and stick the paper in your pants pocket, or stick the paper in the pocket of pants you will be wearing tomorrow. Wherever you are, remember,

"God sent me here."

Struggles, difficulties, and hard times are inevitable. The Bible offers many different names of God to help us love every day, no matter what the circumstances.

Remember the names of God in times of trouble. Which of the following names do you need to remember in your life right now?

Here's some steps to follow:

1. *Circle or highlight* any names of God that you really like or that you want to remember.
2. Then, *look up* all **three** of the verses below the names you highlighted,
3. *Choose one* of the three verses to memorize, and write it in the space provided.
4. *Add the verse* to your memory verses list.
5. *Take your time.* These verses are AWESOME!

Our God

Our Shepherd
>Psalm 23:1
>John 10:11
>Hebrews 13:20

Our Strength & Fortress
>Psalm 22:19
>Jeremiah 16:19a
>Psalm 46:1

Our Helper
>Hebrews 13:6
>Psalm 54:4
>Isaiah 41:10

Our Refuge
>Proverbs 14:26
>Psalm 91:2
>Psalm 46:1

Our Truth
>John 17:17
>1 John 3:19
>John 14:6

Our Father
>1 Peter 4:19
>Psalm 68:5
>John 3:16

Our Guide
>Psalm 25:9
>Psalm 48:14
>Psalm 25:5

Our Peace
>John 14:27
>Philippians 4:6,7
>Proverbs 16:7

Our Rock
>Psalm 62:6
>Psalm 18:2
>2 Samuel 22:3

Our Comforter
>1 Corinthians 1:4
>John 14:26
>Romans 8:1

What? You liked two verses? Sure, here's more room!...

_____

_____

_____

_____

Apply & Obey, Part II
by Chris

Whether it is a prayer in a public school, visibility of the Ten Commandments in a public setting, or a nativity scene, people are taking offense to the name of the Lord, and they seem to be getting the upper hand. We, as Christians, may look on in disbelief, but do we (and are we) standing up for our Lord?

In Genesis 41:16, Joseph also had the opportunity to choose:
> *"So Joseph answered Pharaoh, saying, "It is not in me; God will give Pharaoh an answer of peace."*

Joseph could have taken full credit for interpreting Pharaoh's dream, but **he chose to proclaim the name of the Lord!**

There is a war going on against Christianity, but the devil has *always* waged war to those who believe and proclaim His name. Fellow brothers, we cannot take a laissez-faire attitude toward this battle. Meaning, we are becoming comfortable to let things take their own course without interfering, or without proclaiming the name of our Lord. The **First Book of Corinthians 16:13** says in a straightforward manner,
> *"Watch, stand fast in the faith, be brave, be strong."*

We as Christian men are to be bold in our faith, proclaim His name, and spread His Word!

Copy the previous verse **(1 Corinthians 16:13)** here:

_____

_____

Memorize the verse, and add it to your memory verses list.

Dear Heavenly Father,
Thank You for being our Shepherd, our
Father, our Strength and Fortress; our Helper,
our Peace, our Refuge, and our Rock;
our Truth, and our Comforter!
Amen!

Lesson 2:

He Lives!

Read *Genesis 45:16-28.*

Explanations in your reading:

v. 19- The brothers were given new clothes, wagons, a total of
23 twenty donkeys, each donkey loaded with food, and
Jonathan was given silver.

v. 22 "...three hundred pieces of silver..." Possibly a bit heavier
than a bag of potatoes. The silver provided for Benjamin
and his family (wife and 10 sons – you'll see).

v. 24 "See that you do not become troubled along the way."
NKJV. "Don't quarrel along the way!" NIV, NLT. A lot of
emotions are going on between the brothers, and now they
have a long journey back to Hebron. An argument could easily
flair up about anything. Joseph gave the brothers a wise
reminder to calm down, and have a pleasant trip home.

v. 26 "And Jacob's heart stood still,..." NKJV.
"Jacob was stunned at the news,..." NLT,NIV.
"Jacob's heart fainted..." KJV.

write a summary and your thoughts of the reading:

_____

_____

_____

. . . . .

Reflection of Jesus

He Lives!

Jacob's heart stopped. *"He who was dead now lives."* This is the song that sang in the heart of Jacob! He remembers his son's dreams, the other sons' resentment, and telling Joseph to quiet down. Jacob remembers wondering what *great things* God had planned in Joseph's life…

…then Jacob remembers being handed Joseph's bloody coat.

"How can this be?"

Jacob remembers mourning, "Joseph spoke with so much **hope**, and now he's gone!"

Yet now, Jacob stares at his eleven sons as they tell the good news:

"He's alive!"

Reflection of You

What a feeling! *He who was dead now lives!* This song sang also in the hearts of Jesus' disciples, His followers, and His mother. Like Jacob, they remembered His *promises* of everlasting life. They also, like Jacob, remembered how upset people became as Jesus spoke God's will, and the turmoil and resentment it created. Nonetheless, they found great *hope*, *joy*, and *love* in Jesus' words…

…at least until His blood dripped from His lifeless body on the cross.

"How can this be?"

They grieved, "He spoke with such hope, and now He's gone!"

Yet, on the third day, and even today, those disciples,

His followers, and you and I feel a leap in our hearts as the truth is proclaimed, *"He's alive!"*

Look up **Galatians 2:20.** Write the verse in the space below, and memorize this amazing verse.

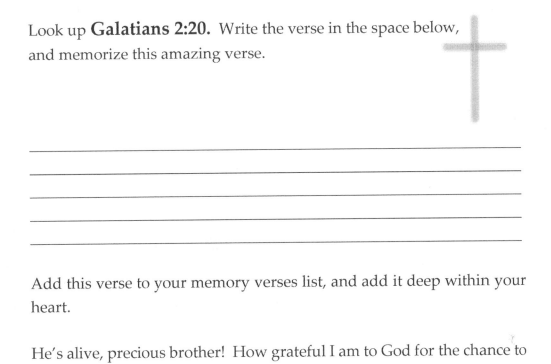

_____

_____

_____

_____

_____

Add this verse to your memory verses list, and add it deep within your heart.

He's alive, precious brother! How grateful I am to God for the chance to proclaim that with you!

Dear Heavenly Father,
Thank You for being Everlasting!
Thank You for the sacrifice of Your
Son, because You love us so much. You alone
give us hope every day. May we remember every
moment that You are our Faithful
God of salvation! We
love You!
Amen.

Chapter 11
The Journey
Genesis 46

I absolutely promise you that there is nothing in this life on this world that will completely equip you with all the knowledge, wisdom, joy, and strength that you will need to grow into a Godly man like trusting in Jesus Christ.

I also promise you that there is no better place in this life to turn to that will give you the encouragement, hope, and direction in any of your confusion like the Bible.

Our Father tells us in Jeremiah 33:3,

> ## *"Come to Me,*
> ## *And I will show you great and mighty things*
> ## *which you do not know."*

So, go to Him. *Go see!*

Lesson 1:
Be Still & Know

Read Genesis 46:1-5.

Explanations on your reading:

v. 2   Israel – remember Israel is the name given to Jacob by God.

v. 3   "...do not fear to go down to Egypt..." Why does God instruct Jacob not to fear? We would think Jacob is excited to go see his son, yet God sees Jacob's heart. Jacob is about to leave the land that God gave to his grandfather Abraham and his father Isaac. Jacob may fear that he is not pleasing God by leaving.

v. 4   "...I will bring you up again..." God is explaining to Jacob, "Don't worry, all your descendants will be back one day living in the land."

v.4   "Joseph will put his hand on your eyes." NKJV, KJV. "...close your eyes..." NIV NAS. God is assuring the truth to Jacob that his beloved son Joseph will be by his side for the rest of Jacob's life.

write a summary and your own thoughts of the reading:

_____

_____

_____

. . . . .

Beersheba

The Wilderness of Beersheba is where God provided Hagar (Sarah's servant – Joseph's great grandmother) and her son Ishmael with water when he was dying (Genesis 21:14). Beersheba was named by Abraham, after making a covenant with King Abimelech of Gerar, which is Philistine territory (Genesis 21:31).

Beersheba is also where God appeared to Isaac, Jacob's father, and said to Isaac, *"I am the God of your father Abraham; do not fear; for I am with you. I will bless you and multiply your descendants for My servant Abraham's sake"* *(Genesis 26:23,24).*

Beersheba has been a special place to Jacob down through the years, and special to his father Isaac and to his grandfather Abraham. Now, with a joyful, elated heart, Jacob is travelling to Egypt to see his beloved son, and he comes to that special place, Beersheba. In Beersheba, Jacob stops his travelling to thank God.

Remember Beersheba when mentioned in the Bible. Find it on the map in the appendix. Be familiar with where it is located. It was a special place to Abraham and his descendants.

What place in your own life is special? What, and where is your own personal "Beersheba"? Why is it special? What happened there?

_____

_____

_____

Israel (Jacob) stopped to offer sacrifices to God. He stopped his exciting journey, not just to rest, but to remember God by offering a sacrifice.

Offering a sacrifice? Like an animal?

Lifestyles are different today and continue to change. Let us try to get an understanding of this practice. The first sacrifice in the Bible was by God in Genesis 3:21. He clothed and covered Adam and Eve, because of the sin. They were clothed in animal skin; therefore, an animal was sacrificed.

A sacrifice is giving away something that God gave us that is important to us in our daily lives. Sacrificing is having an understanding that although we may be affected by the loss, God's kingdom and His will in our lives is still strong and powerful. Therefore, we sacrifice cheerfully and in worship.

Here, Jacob sacrificed an animal. Jacob's way of living was so different compared to our way of living today. Most of us do not depend on the farm animals in our pasture to feed us and our families, and clothe us. No, we typically take a small travel, not by foot either, to the nearest grocery store. Therefore, when we think of the sacrifice of a goat or a sheep, it can be difficult for us to see that this was really a big deal. Giving up anything that is important to us is a sacrifice.

Israel (Jacob) loved God so much. He was willing to stop his exciting journey of seeing his beloved son Joseph. He was willing to *stop*, not just to rest, but to rest in the LORD, and to give his heart to God. Then Jacob completely leaned on God. He stopped what he was doing for God alone!

The BEST part about it is that Israel *stopped* long enough to hear the voice of God.

When we make time for God, we just have to **stop** – **stop** our feet from moving, **stop** our pencils, **stop** our talking, **stop** our thoughts from racing around in our heads, and focus just on God, *what His word says*, and Who He is.

After all, how can we listen to God if our hands, feet, mouth, or our mind is moving about?

Look up **Matthew 7:24**, write the verse in the space below, and memorize it:

_____

_____

_____

Remember to add the verse to your memory verses list.

Dear Heavenly Father,
Thank you for being Faithful. Help us
to remember that You have words of life
for us to hear.
Amen.

Lesson 2:
Meet the Family

Read Genesis 46:6-30.

(Don't let your tongue get tied to your lips trying to pronounce all the names! Do your best and move on.)

Write a summary and your own thoughts of the reading:

_____

_____

_____

• • • • •

Verses 9 through 27 give many names of all the children, grandchildren, and great-grandchildren of Jacob. It gives historical information.

To make this reading easier, really fun, and interesting, do the following:

1. **Underline** the names of all the sons of Jacob, including his daughter Dinah's (v. 15) name. Here are the names to look for:

Reuben-v.9	Issachar-v.13	Joseph-v.20,27
Simeon-v.10	Zebulun-v.14	Benjamin-v.21
Levi-v.11	Gad-v.16	Dan-v.23
Judah-v.12	Asher-v.17	Naphtali-v.24.

2. **Count** the number of **sons and daughters** each brother had. Place the number beside the father's name that you underlined. For example, in your Bible where you underlined Reuben, place the

number "4" beside his name (in verse 9), because Reuben had four sons.

3. Verse 12 can get complicated. Judah had 5 children, and 2 grandchildren. However, 2 of Judah's children died. He had 5 children, minus 2 children, plus 2 grandchildren (5-2+2=5); therefore, **place a "5" by Judah's name.**

4. Still in verse 12, highlight, place a star, or draw a cross by Judah, Perez, and Hezron. They are descendants of Jesus Christ!

5. Similarly, in verse 17, Asher's son Beriah had 2 children, giving Asher 5 children and 2 grandchildren; therefore, **place a "7" by Asher's name.**

6. **Add up** all the numbers you have written down beside each name. You should have **70 total.** Didn't work out? It didn't for me the first time either. *You will find this in the appendix all laid out for you!*

7. Circle the number 70 in verse 27. Now you can actually picture Jacob and all of his family moving. Now that is some serious Bible-digging! Good work, brother!

Dear Heavenly Father,
Thank You for being the
Author of the Word of Life! How
great and infallible is Your Word!
Amen.

Lesson 3:
Different

Read *Genesis 46:31-34.*

Write a summary and your own thoughts of the reading:

_____

_____

_____

. . . . .

Goshen is on the map in the appendix. It is not in the middle of Egypt, but to the side, closest to Canaan. Jacob and all the family were coming to *live* in Egypt, not to invade Egypt, and not to become Egyptians.

The family of Jacob stayed to the side, in Goshen, and remained

shepherds. They did not pick up the Egyptian culture, or worship their gods, and it is doubtful any of Joseph's brothers started wearing make-up and gold jewelry. Jacob and his family were different, and they respectfully stayed to the side.

Look up and read **Psalm 1:1.**

Now circle the correct answers to the following questions:

1. Verse one guides us to
    a. never walk with ungodly people, or
    b. never walk *in the way* of ungodly people (never take their advice).

2. Verse one also states that we should not
   a. stand with sinners, or
   b. stand *in the path* of sinners (see things as sinners do).

3. Lastly, verse one advises that we not
   a. sit with the scornful, or mockers, or
   b. sit *in the seat* of the scornful, or mocker, (participating in their hateful attitude).

Hopefully, you circled "b" in each one. Did you find this tricky? It is important that we do not shun away sinners and the lost. At the same time, it is important that we do not keep company with sinners and the lost at such an extent that we start to think, speak, and act in their manner.

I can show love, care, concern, an open ear, a smile, and my own salvation with someone who lives contrary to Biblical teaching; however, I have to be careful not to take the person's advice for my own life, or stay in their home, or go with them to live their way.

It is always easier to pull someone down than to pull someone up. As a result, we as devoted Christians must stay out of the way, out of the path, and out of the seat, continuously and humbly loving, praying, and reaching out for the lost.

Dear Heavenly Father,
Thank You for being our Shepherd.
Guide us in discerning what is truth
and what is false.
May we obey Your Holy Word.
Amen.

Chapter 12
Life in Egypt
Genesis 47

New beginnings are exciting and scary at the same time. Some beginnings are simple, like a new friendship, and others are more complex, like a new school or home.

God has many new beginnings planned for you. Some may seem overwhelming, but do not fear. These new beginnings are an opportunity for you to grow, to do things even better, and to excitingly see how God reveals His plan for your life. My brother, these plans are filled with good things and hope (Jeremiah 29:11).

Every single morning, God has all new love to give you! There is something else from God's heart that He wants you to remember:

"Behold, I will do a new thing, now it shall spring forth,
Shall you not know it? I will even make a road in the
wilderness
And rivers in the desert…"
Isaiah 43:19

Lesson 1:
The Pilgrim

Read Genesis 47:1-12.

Explanation in your reading:

> v. 7 "…Jacob blessed the Pharaoh…" Jacob may have given a gift to Pharaoh, a greeting, words of wisdom, a prayer, or inspiration.

Write a summary and your own thoughts of the reading:

_____

_____

_____

· · · · · ·

When Pharaoh asked Jacob how old he was, Jacob described his 130 years as *few* and *evil*. He also calls his life a *pilgrimage*.

"Few." Living over 100 years does not sound like a few days, especially when we look back on Jacob's life…

- He was born a twin, and was completely opposite from his twin brother Esau.
- Jacob lied horribly to his blind father Isaac, pretending to be Esau.
- Jacob dreamed of a ladder climbing up to heaven.
- Jacob wrestled, literally, with God. God dislocated Jacob's hip.
- God gives Jacob the name Israel.
- Jacob fell in love with Rachel and worked 14 years in her father's fields to marry her.
- Jacob married sisters Leah and Rachel, and had 13 children.

- Jacob reconciled with his brother Esau.
- Jacob buried his father.
- Jacob mourned his wife Rachel's death as she gave birth to Benjamin.
- Jacob took the time to make a beautiful coat of many colors for his most beloved son Joseph.
- Jacob greatly mourned the supposed death of Joseph.

These events in Jacob's life seem like more than just a few days, don't they? But they are just a few days compared to *eternity.* Considering Jacob had such a close, personal relationship with God, Jacob understood that eternal life was much greater.

Look up **Psalm 144:4**, and write the verse below:

_____

_____

_____

Memorize the verse, and add it to your memory verses list.

"Evil." Perhaps Jacob's life, or our own lives, do not seem evil when we think about them, but if we compare our present lives to eternal life in Heaven with our Heavenly Father, there is really a *big difference.* The blessings that God gives us now are wonderful, and they provide us with a beauty in this life. Ultimately, I believe they are tiny glimpses of what we have to look forward to in Heaven.

Every good and perfect gift is from above. James 1:17

God is guiding us to keep our focus on eternity! Therefore, *we are pilgrims!*

"But lay up for yourselves treasures in heaven..."
Matthew 6:20

"Pilgrimage." As followers of Jesus Christ, we follow God's will, and prepare to meet our Savior one day.

*Be watchful, stand firm in the faith, act like men, be
strong.
1 Corinthians 16:13 ESV*

Until then, enjoy the journey – Jesus *wants* you to enjoy your life as a pilgrim.

Look up **John 16:33**, and write the verse below:

_____

_____

_____

_____

Memorize this verse! Hide it in your heart!

When we keep our focus on spending eternity in Heaven, these days of life-long travel do seem few, and God's goodness and blessings leave the rest of the world "evil."

Dear Heavenly Father,
Thank You for being Eternal!
May our lives here on earth be fruitful
and joyful as we prepare for the fruits and joys
You are preparing for us in Heaven!
Amen.

Reflection of Jesus

Pilgrimage

Isaac, Joseph's grandfather, most likely God's promise of living in the land of Canaan one day, or Israel, and living as saints of God in eternity forever.

"God has a plan for you." Joseph heard these words spoken by his father and grandfather; however, how easy was that for Joseph to believe as he was dragged away from his family to a foreign land, or when he was a prisoner, falsely accused and forgotten about? I imagine he was confused, angry, and terrified; yet, only to a particular *point*. Joseph's hope and faith in eternity with God eased and calmed his emotions, attitude, and fears about his present situations. He would *"not perish, but have everlasting life."*

The reason Jesus was born as a baby on earth was to die, and then raise from the dead and live forever. He knew His life on earth was temporary, and His life in Heaven would be forever. Therefore, the peace of His faith and His understanding of pilgrimage flooded all thoughts of fear or hopelessness.

Reflection of You

Our character is not found in the good things we do, and not when we feel our strength is strong; but when situations seem hopeless, and when we feel weak. Our character ends at the point we say, "Forget it," or "I quit," or "It's hopeless," or "I give up."

154

God allows us to go through hard times to show us where we need to rely on Him and keep our faith strong in Him (not just in ourselves). God does have a plan for you, dear brother, and it all points to eternity.

"... we also glory in tribulations, knowing that tribulation produces perseverance; and perseverance, character, and character, hope."
Romans 5:3,4

Lesson 2:
Stewardship

Read *Genesis 47:13-31.*

Explanations in your reading:

v. 29 "...please put your hand under my thigh." This was a tradition of how an oath, or a promise, was made.

v. 28 "Jacob lived in the land of Egypt for 17 years." This means the famine was over long before Jacob died; therefore, the entire family had the blessed fortune to celebrate together when the 7 years of famine was over, and RAIN came pouring from the sky!

v. 31 Israel (Jacob) bows himself on the head of the bed. He is praying.

Write a summary and your own thoughts of the reading:

_____

_____

_____

• • • • •

A sizable amount of information in these verses sustains the importance of writing summaries. Here are the facts we learn in these verses:

1. Because of the famine, **everyone is out of food** – Canaan, Egypt, and their neighboring lands.

2. **Joseph gathered money** from the Egyptians to give to the Pharaoh -- a *tax*, where the citizens give money to the government to help support an entire community or country.

3. **The money failed!** They could not eat their money, so their money was worthless – it failed.

156

4. **Livestock held greater value.** What little livestock that was left was traded in for **bread** that had previously been stored. This is how they ate for *a whole year!*

5. The next year, **all livestock becomes property of the Pharaoh.** The people have nothing left to give besides *themselves* and their land. Verse 20 states Joseph "bought the l and," meaning he did not just take it. The Egyptians and Canaanites were paid for their land.

6. **Joseph orders all people to leave their homes and move closer to *the city*.** Why? All the *livestock* is in the cities and must be cared for, and the land is now of no value; therefore, it is more convenient to move closer to the food supply located in the cities. Also, a greater amount of people in one place could mean *greater commerce*, meaning now selling, buying, and trading are more convenient and easier.

Life-changing events pound on the Egyptians! In the midst of the severe famine and the draining storehouses, people realize that everyone is being affected – not just the poor, not just the rich, *everyone!*

Joseph gives the people seeds to plant and grow their own crops. Since the land now belongs to Pharaoh, Joseph can oversee that the people are being responsible in planting the seed and providing their own food again for their families. Small streams and dying creeks of the Nile River and the Delta were most likely the only water supplies.

Verse 26 tells us that one-fifth of the harvest was given to Pharaoh. Why? (See Genesis 41:34)

_____

_____

Joseph had good stewardship, and was therefore able to solve any dilemma, and provide for the country of Egypt.

Apply & Obey

Look up **Proverb 27:23**, and write the verse in the space below:

_____

_____

_____

Memorize this verse, and add it in your memory verses list. *You are going to need to have this verse in your heart to help you grow into a financially stable, godly man.*

Yes, I am aware that you are probably not a shepherd, and that you may be wondering, "Why do I need to memorize a verse that tells me to take care of my flock?' Your flock can be anything in your possession that you care for and tend to, such as money and time.

Now, look up the word stewardship, and write the definition in the space below:

Stewardship-

_____

_____

_____

Suppose you are given $100.00, and you ask *me* to hold on to it for you. Sometime later, you need your $100.00 back, and you ask me for it. Then, I reply, "What money? Oh, that? I dunno. I think I spent it all. You gave it to me, right?"

Yikes! You expected and trusted me to be a *good steward* of your money, and I blew it! You trusted me with what you gave me, but it was still *your* money!

When God gives us money, days, health, and other wonderful things, these blessings are all from GOD, and all these things still belong to GOD! God owns what I have, and I am to be a good steward with what *He* owns. We have what we have so that God can do His will in our lives.

For of Him and through Him and to Him are all things,
to whom be glory forever.
Amen.
Romans 11:36

Our goal in life should not be to have lots of money, but our goal in life should be to do God's will with what we have, no matter how much or how little that may be. Remember that **Ephesians 3:20** encourages us,

Now to Him who is able to do exceedingly abundantly
above all that we ask or think according to the power that
works in us.
Ephesians 3:20

Exceedingly abundantly above all!!! Wow! It sounds like you and I sure are cared for, brother, and always will be! There is no need to worry about being rich enough. Our Father has it all under His control.

· · · · ·

Apply & Obey

Practice good stewardship starting today! The envelope system is a great way to practice stewardship. Start by finding three envelopes. Each envelope needs a name. Here are the 3 names to write on the front of each envelope:

- "$ to give"
- "$ to save"
- "$ to spend"

Also, write your name on each envelope, but do not write, "My Money," because remember, it's really God's money. You are the steward.

Then add a small piece of paper to each envelope, about the size of a bookmark. On this paper, you will log the date, and how much money goes into the envelope, and/or how much money comes out, something like this:

<u>Date</u>   <u>Deposit/Debit</u>   <u>Total</u>

Keep these three envelopes together, and keep the three envelopes in a secure place, such as a manila folder, a shoebox, a sock drawer, or a desk drawer.

With your three envelopes, keep a piece of notebook paper with the title, *"My Financial Goals: How does God want me to glorify Him with my money?"*

Think about what you would like to do with the money that you save, spend, and give: save for a new bike, give more to your church, save for a summer camp, buy your parent or grandparent a present, buy yourself something special, save for Christmas presents, give to a missionary, save for a mission trip, save for a future car, deposit in your bank account,... Pray about it, be sure about it, and write it down. Then, stay focused on your goals as you add money to (or take money out of) your envelopes.

If you regularly carry a wallet, you may choose to place your spending money in your wallet rather than in your "$ to spend" envelope. However, keep the spending envelope with your other envelopes. It can come in handy when you do not want to spend *all* your spending money at one time, and you may be tempted if you are carrying it all at the same time.

The envelope system is a popular way to be responsible with money, but it takes discipline and dedication. Talk to your parents about the money system. Ask them to hold you accountable and guide you along the way.

Dear Heavenly Father,
Thank You for being our Provider.
Guide us to be good stewards with all
You trust us with.
Amen.

Chapter 13
Time with Dad
Genesis 48

In Genesis 48, Jacob is now 147 years old, and Joseph is 57. This father-son duo is getting older. Joseph's sons, Manasseh and Ephraim, are now adults.

All of Jacob's sons are still living. Considering God gave Jacob the name Israel, the twelve sons, who are forming bigger families, or tribes, are *Israelites*. They will forever, even today, be known as **the twelve tribes of Israel**.

Oh, how small days can change the big world! How a small prayer can birth big healing. How a small smile can boost big encouragement. How this small moment in your life right now can enlighten and activate the big love in your heart!

This moment is never small!

Lesson 1:
Meet Granddad

Read *Genesis 48:1-12.*

Explanations in your reading:

v. 3   *"God Almighty came to me..."* See Luz on the map in the Appendix. The life event that Israel is telling Joseph about is found in Genesis 28:10-17. What an amazing life event for a father to share with his son!

v. 5, 16   *"...your two sons...are mine..."* A huge proclamation made by Israel! Israel is telling Joseph that Manasseh and Ephraim are equal to Jacob's other sons now, such as Reuben and Simeon. Therefore, these two boys will **not** be heirs to the Egyptian throne – they will not follow in their father Joseph's footsteps. As Jacob commands, Manasseh and Ephraim are not to be rich Egyptian politicians. These boys are to be descendants of Abraham, heirs to the promised land of Canaan, and leaders of their own tribes/families.

Write a summary and your own thoughts of the reading:

_____

_____

_____

•   •   •   •   •

Ephraim and Manasseh were no longer known as the sons of an Egyptian legend. They were now to be known as descendants of Israel, carrying the name *Israel*. Therefore, they **represented** this name, like a reflection, the way water reflects the mountains around the pond.

What does it mean to **represent** a name?

_____

_____

_____

_____

If anyone wanted to know more about the people of Israel, that person should have been able to look at and watch any descendant of Israel, including Manasseh and Ephraim, and then they would know.

If anyone wants to know anything about **your father**, or your grandfather, or your family, they can look at you or watch you, and then they should know.

If anyone wants to know what **Jesus** is like, they *should* be able to look at us, and watch us, and then they will know.

To help you see how you represent Jesus, think of what it is like to represent your father.

If I choose to sin with no care of what others think or see, I am pointing a distasteful picture of my earthly dad, and I am giving him a bad name. *You* represent *your* earthly God-given father, your dad! You represent his name. When my own children are in public or anywhere outside the house, they represent the name **Foster**.

Whether or not you believe your own earthly dad is a good man, or  whether or not he is a Christian man has nothing to do with it. While we cannot control our dads' actions, we can control how we reflect and revere his name, because worthiness is there!

Listen carefully, your earthly dad is worthy for **3** big reasons:

1. Exodus 20:12 instructs us to HONOR our father and mother;
2. *You* were created by God from your earthly father; AND
3. God assigned this man to be your earthly dad, and God assigned you to be this man's son, and ***GOD MAKES NO MISTAKES!***

How proud and joyful any father will be knowing you honor his name and that you work so hard to see that his name is honored. It is a wonderful act to do for your dad. It shows him that you have not and will not forget him. It shows him that you hold his name in high regard. It shows him that you want others to know that you love him and you are his son. With all this honor to your dad, he just might even swell up a tear. For your dad to see you caring about your name probably floods his heart so intimately with joy, and the glory and the will of God can beam through that awesome father-son relationship.

Walk in reverence and honor of your dad, and it will give you a better understanding of how to walk in reverence and honor of your Heavenly Dad. Flood *God's* heart with joy, too!

If you carry the name of Jesus, you represent Jesus. You represent your Heavenly Father.

To *represent* means to reflect, to be like, or to show others what someone or something is like.

If we proclaim to be Christian, and then we point our fingers at a sinner, or we show bad manners or say bad words, or we do not forgive, someone is going to believe that Jesus points fingers, and that Jesus' teachings do not work. People are watching when we represent *and* misrepresent!

When we reflect Jesus, we try to be like Him, and we try to show others what Jesus is like. Perhaps we show more care for others, and are more kind to others. We are careful not to boast, and careful not to judge. Then, hopefully, others will see that Jesus is a really great name!

As a man of God, you have two huge names to carry. Carry them in honor, in humility, and in reverence.

Look up **1 Peter 3:15,** and write the verse below.

_____

_____

_____

_____

Memorize this verse, and add it to your memory verses list.

Dear Heavenly Father,
Thank You for being just that – my
Father! Thank You for the dad that you
gave me. Protect him, love him, and guide him
closer to you. Show me how to always hold
his name high, and how to hold
Your Name high.
Amen.

Lesson 2:
The "Hand-Off"

Read *Genesis 48:13-22.*

Explanations in your reading:

v. 13 "...Ephraim with his right hand toward Israel's left hand, and Manasseh with his left hand toward Israel's right hand..." Like this:

v. 14 "Then Israel stretched out his..." Israel either crisscrossed his hands, like below, or had his grandsons switch places:

Israel may have resituated where the grandsons were standing, so that he could reach them easier.

These two brothers, Manasseh and Ephraim, are going through a similar ritual that their grandfather Israel and their great-uncle Esau experienced (see Genesis 27). The younger brother is receiving the blessing that traditionally and rightfully belongs to the oldest brother.

> v. 21 "…God…will bring you back to the land of your fathers." Joseph's *descendants* will see the land promised by God (Book of Joshua), but not Joseph himself.

> v. 22 "I have given you…" Ephraim and Manasseh will acquire the most land in the promised land of Israel. The back of your own Bible should have a map showing territory of each of the twelve tribes.

Write a summary and your own thoughts of the reading:

_____

_____

_____

. . . . .

Do you remember the meanings of Manasseh's name and Ephraim's name? How Joseph named his children reflects his heart:

- *Manasseh:* "For God has made me forget all my toil and all my father's house."
- *Ephraim:* "For God has caused me to be fruitful in the land of my affliction."

Joseph found comfort in *knowing* and *understanding* that God *heals every heart!* God wants you to have your own form of Manasseh and Ephraim in your own life.

Let us start with our **Manasseh:**

Although it is difficult to let go of and forget the unfortunate event(s) of your past, it's time to work through that now! Read the following verses:

170

Do not remember the former things,
Nor consider the things of old.
Behold, I will do a new thing,
Now it shall spring forth;
Shall you not know it?
I will even make a road in the wilderness
And rivers in the desert.
Isaiah 43:18,19

Therefore, if anyone is in Christ, he is a new creation; old things have passed away; behold, all things have become new.
2 Corinthians 5:17

But one thing I do, forgetting those things which are behind and reaching forward to those things which are ahead.
Philippians 3:13

Choose one of the three verses you just read, one that you believe God wants you to memorize and hide in your heart, and write the verse on the next page:

_____

_____

_____

_____

Forgetting the bad things of your pass will not cause you to have another day like it. Like Joseph, God wants to help you forget the bad days and keep looking ahead. LET GO of what saddened you in the past, what angered you, what bothered you, what gave you stress. Stamp the word MANASSEH over these things.

These bad memories are a burden that weigh you down and keep you from giving God your whole heart! Besides, God is bigger than your toils. You know this, but "AMEN" to being reminded!

Now on to **Ephraim:**

There is no Ephraim (God making fruitful) without Manasseh (forgetting my toil). We cannot follow God and constantly think of the negative things in our life. It's true. The Bible says so:

- In Genesis 19:26, Lot's wife *looked back* at their old city of sin, and turned into a pillar of salt for doing so!
- In Luke 9:62, Jesus explains that one must *not look back* at his old life to follow Him.

172

- In Matthew 10:14, Jesus explains to the disciples to not let anyone make them feel bad or unworthy and *"shake off the dust from your feet."*

So as you can see, God wants us to keep moving forward so that we can see the amazing, wonderful, beautiful things HE has planned for us.

In so many ways, God has already made you fruitful! He has equipped you with strengths, gifts, talents, and bunches of blessings! What are they? List as many as you can think of here, just to brighten your day:

_____

_____

_____

_____

_____

_____

Like Joseph, God is with you. That is an *awesome* blessing! The redemption of our sins on the cross AND the resurrection of our Lord and Savior are also *awesome* blessings! Dear brother, you are soaked with blessings! *SOAKED!*

Dear Heavenly Father,
Thank you for being our Shepherd.
You keep us moving forward in this life, and
You flood us with blessings, all because
You love us. We love You, too!
Amen.

Chapter 14
Worth of Words
Genesis 49

Whatever is going on in our heads and in our hearts certainly is reflected in our words. If I know nothing about you, just speak to me, and I can learn so much more than just the words you say. I learn a thought or two that you have, maybe your attitude, what you believe, and something that you like and don't like. All of this is exposed without you having to tell me.

In Chapter 49, Israel's heart is exposed. In other words, we see his faith in God, his close relationship with God, and his full surrender to God's plan; all of this, without Israel saying so, just by the words he says.

May our own words and thoughts give glory to God.

Let the words of my mouth and the meditation of my heart be
acceptable in Your sight, O LORD, my strength and my Redeemer.
Psalm 19:14

Lesson 1:
Spirit-Led Words

Read Genesis 49:1-21.

This chapter begins with Jacob on his deathbed, gathering all of his twelve sons together so that he can give them blessings. A father's blessings before his death were revered, with great magnitude in everyone's lives. The words were sealed, as commandments.

To make this reading easier, try these steps:
1. Circle each name, starting with Reuben.
2. Underline words that Israel uses to describe each son, such as "excellency of dignity," or "unstable as water."
3. Draw squiggly lines (like this) under all words that give future blessings, such as "you shall not excel."
4. Bookmark the map in your own Bible that shows the territories that each son actually possesses. Probably titled, "Tribes of Israel."
5. Refer to the "Explanations in your reading" as you read about each brother. I gave each verse an explanation as I studied it and felt led by God to see it. If you consider this part of our Bible reading difficult, I agree with you.

Explanations in your reading:

v. 4 "...you went up to your father's bed..." NKJV. See Genesis 35:22.

v. 6 "...they slew a man..." NKJV. See Genesis 34:25-30.

v. 10 "The scepter shall not depart from Judah." NKJV A scepter is the type of staff carried by kings. It signifies royalty. **Judah's** ascendant will be the King of Kings, Jesus Christ.

v. 13 Although the territory of **Zebulun** never touched the sea, it is interesting that *Nazareth* is in this territory, where the One who calmed the sea grew up!

v. 15 "**Issachar**...and became a band of slaves." Issachar territory had good land and produced good crops, which would keep Issacharites busy. 1 Chronicles 12 describes the Issachar tribe as knowledgeable and competent. The Issacharites were also good learners.

v. 16 "**Dan**...a viper..." I agree that Dad's (Israel's) compliments seem a bit strange. Nevertheless, *my own* explanation here involves a man from the tribe of Dan, *(Samson)* hundreds of years later, who cunningly (as a *snake*) destroyed the temple by pushing down the pillars, killing all Philistines inside the temple. *I* believe Jacob was prophesizing greatness of Dan's tribe.

v. 18 "I have waited for your salvation, O LORD!" Israel is taking a moment to praise God and give God thanks for speaking through him to his sons.

v. 19 "**Gad**, a troop..." Gad is encouraged to persevere. Elijah the prophet was from the Gad tribe.

v. 20 "Bread from **Asher**..." The Asher territory is located on the Mediterranean Sea, opening the tribe of Asher up to much trade; and therefore, giving the tribe of Asher much wealth. Sounds nice, but worldly possessions rot, mold, and rust.

v. 21 **Naphtali**...a deer..." This blessing can be interpreted in several ways. One city in the Naphtali territory is Capernaum, where Jesus spent time teaching.

Write a summary and your own thoughts of the reading:

_____

_____

_____

_____

· · · · ·

These words of Jacob are remembered and obeyed over 400 years later, when Joshua and the Israelites are dividing up the land of Canaan.

Moses, the "co-author"

God commanded Moses to write down the events that took place as he and the other Israelites wandered through the Wilderness of Paran.

- Exodus 12:14 are God's words to Moses, "Moses, write this down..."
- In Exodus 24:4, "Moses wrote all the words of the LORD."
- In Exodus 34:27, "Then the LORD said to Moses, 'Write these words.'"
- Exodus 31:22: "So it was, when Moses had completed writing the words of this law in a book, when they were finished,..."

There are many more verses that explain Moses obeying God and writing Genesis, Exodus, Leviticus, and Deuteronomy. Our entire Bible study is based on Moses' obedience to God to write the words.

In Joshua 8:32-35, Joshua carefully wrote a copy of Moses' writings, without a word missing.

178

So as you can see, the Word of God as given to Moses is now being passed down, copied, and spread to other people.

Was Moses the only one that knew of Abraham, Adam, Eve, Noah, Esau, Jacob, and Joseph? No way! Think about who was with Moses – the tribes of the twelve sons of Israel! These family members knew the stories and happenings of their own families. These important events were definitely passed down, and Moses had much knowledge of the past. *However*, the Bible was written by the power of God; they were *"God-breathed," perfect, mistake-free, infallible.*

I pray that you always love the sweet words of your Bible. Genesis 49 is a *tough* chapter to read, but you now have a great knowledge of the tribes which are mentioned again and again all throughout the Bible, all the way to Revelation! What's more, God is well pleased that you *took the time* to get to know Him!

Dear Heavenly Father,
Thank You for being the
Author of our salvation! Your word is
Truth, powerful, healing, a light unto our path,
and a lamp unto our feet!
May I always hunger for
Your Word!
Amen.

Lesson 2:

A Father's Last Words

Read Genesis 49:22-33.

Explanations in your reading:

v. 22-26   A bough is a tree branch, stronger than a twig or small limb. Part of the tree. Jacob takes the time to let Joseph know that he is proud of him. Manasseh and Ephraim are given large territories in Israel.

v. 27   **Benjamin**...a ravenous wolf..." Remember that Israel is not speaking of Benjamin himself so much as he is speaking of Benjamin's descendants. King Saul was from the tribe of Benjamin, as well as the apostle Paul in the Book of Acts.

v. 33   "...and was gathered to his people." NKJV. "...joined ancestors in death." NIV. Jacob was not buried yet. When he breathed his last breath, he was present with Abraham, Sarah, Isaac, Rebekah, Leah, and Rachel, who all died before him. This verse gives us insight to what happens when we die.

Write a summary and your own thoughts of the reading:

_____

_____

_____

·   ·   ·   ·   ·

Jacob saw that God's hands were at work in Joseph's life.

Jacob is telling Joseph, "My blessings from God are so great because I have you as my son." What love! This father and son had a pure and loving relationship.

I imagine they both gazed lovingly at each other as Jacob spoke. So much love poured out by both, and knowing that Jacob is about to die. I imagine God's presence was so powerful that all those who were near could feel His presence and His glory, hovering over as if ready to lead Jacob on home.

When a saint is about to die, God really is magnified. The ugly dark realization of death never clouds out the hope and faith of believers in Jesus Christ.

An example in my own life is my grandmother, or "Grandma," who lay dying in the hospital at age 92. All her daughters, including my mother, gathered around her bed and sang some of Grandma's favorite old hymnals, one after another. With a room full of praise to God, HE was magnified! Not death, not sadness, not grief, but God was our focus. Even on Grandma's old dying face, I could see hope and her anticipated joy to be led home by Jesus.

I

believe those standing near Jacob could see the same thing on Jacob's old, dying face. These twelve sons remembered, deep within their hearts, their father's last words.

Being a Christian is packed full with hope. We will be together again in eternity. Grasp and gaze at that hope.

Look up **Philippians 3:20**, and write the verses below:

_____

_____

_____

_____

_____

Memorize this verse, and add it to your memory verses list.

Dear Heavenly Father,
Thank You for being
Everlasting! Thank You for the hope
You give us through the Resurrection
of Jesus Christ to live with You forever!
Amen.

Chapter 15

The Inevitable

Genesis 50

May I be the first to congratulate you on making it to the last chapter of Genesis! This has not been an easy journey, but you have dug through so much of God's Word, persevering through some tough reading of so long ago.

I believe God intended for the reading of Joseph's life in Genesis to reflect *life*. Every day is not always great. Sometimes, we have to stop and figure things out before we move on. Life, like Genesis, is packed full with new things to learn about wisdom, truth, and God.

Make the most of the information in the appendix when you finish this chapter. Continue to hold tight to the Word of God. Check out all the maps and extra information given in your own Bible. Also, after you finish this study, keep your memory verses close to you.

Lesson 1:
The D Word

Read *Genesis 50:1-14.*

Write a summary and your own thoughts of the reading:

_____

_____

_____

. . . . .

Then Joseph wept. The hardest and saddest times of life are seeing **death**, particularly the death of a family member. It is not wrong to be sad and cry when someone dies. God gave us tear ducts in our eyes for a reason. So it is understandable to be sad and feel lonely at these times.

You also know that death is inevitable – we cannot escape it. With life is death. They go hand-in-hand. You cannot have one without the other. How do you feel about that? Most likely, as anyone, you find it terrifying and fearful.

By knowing Jesus Christ (the King of all and everything) as your Lord (the leader of your life) and Savior (He died in your place because of your sins, then rose again eternally to give you eternal life), you will have a peace and even joy in everything, in tough times, and even in experiences with death. There is peace because we remember to turn to God.

In obituaries today, a person who has died is proclaimed as "deceased." Also included is a birth date, a hyphen, then a death date, like this: "01-02-1903 – 02-03-2004."

One day, I did some digging pertaining to my own ancestors. I found the obituary of my great-great-great grandfather, named Absalom. The newspaper column read, "Physician states reason for death: "God's appointed time."

God's appointed time! Today, the world gives no recognition in newspapers to *God* when someone dies or when someone is born. God is given no credit in most of the world. How horribly sad. The Maker, who proclaims in Isaiah 44:24, *"I am the LORD, who makes all things,"* is left out!

The Bible also tells us to pray, "Thy kingdom come." God wants us to pray and wait for His return, and to base our whole lives on that special moment when we see His loving face.

Considering all things are of God and through God and to God, this includes every aspect of our lives, AND every aspect of death. So, my precious brother, He is always there and always *in control*, for eternity.

In these living fleshly bodies, it is hard to think of forever and eternity. Our fleshly bodies are not equipped for eternity because of our sin-filled lives; therefore, these bodies have an end. Yet our lives surrendered to Christ give us new bodies and new life.
In **John 14:3,** Jesus promises,
"And if I go and prepare a place for you, I will come again and receive you to Myself, that where I am, there you may be also."

In thinking about this life, and death, Heaven, eternity, God's will, and your relationship with Christ, write out your own prayer to God. Share

187

your heart, your thoughts, your griefs, your questions, and your gratitude and praise.

Lesson 2:
Forgiveness

Read *Genesis 50:15-19.*

Write a summary and your own thoughts of the reading:

_____

_____

_____

• • • • •

Joseph now has the chance to get back at his brothers for treating him so cruelly. Yet, he chooses to love them, to care for them, and to be kind to them. Joseph chose *God first*, before his hurt feelings and anger. Joseph's faith in God pushed away thoughts of revenge.

He could have given them an evil look, the cold shoulder, or he could have just ignored them. Yet, **he did not!** These acts of retaliation were not God's will, just as he told his brothers, "...**am I in the place of God?**"

Have you ever hit back, talked back, tattled, or glared at someone in disapproval? Have you ever felt like you needed to teach someone a lesson, and make them pay back with the wrath of *you*? I will admit it – I sure have! Through my experience in this sin, I realize it is the wrong choice.

> Do not say, "I will repay evil";
> wait for the LORD, and he will deliver you.
> Proverbs 20:22

When we hold on to a hurt by not forgiving, we are hurting ourselves. We lock up our joy.

Unforgiving is a heavy weight, and it locks up *your* joy, not another's joy. If you forgive, it will release you from that dark, heavy grudge.

Forgiving is a choice you make. It is *not* a feeling. You do not just start feeling better around the person who wronged you, and then decide to forgive him/her. With full awareness and in prayer to God, forgive this person of their debt, AND ask God to forgive this person. It is worship and reverence to God, because you realize Jesus died for *this* person, too, and needs forgiveness. We don't have the authority to say someone should not be forgiven.

It is the *forgiveness* that lifts the weight, not a *feeling*!

Dear brother in Christ, the Holy Spirit equips us to worship God in this way and will guide us along the way.

When we show kindness to those that have wronged us, we are trusting God, and having faith in His plan.

In **Matthew 5:44**, Jesus gives us a way to worship when we are wronged:

"But I say to you, love your enemies, bless those who curse you, do good to those who hate you, and pray for those who spitefully use you and persecute you."

Copying a verse helps us focus on it and helps to memorize it; therefore, write the verse from your own Bible version, or copy the NKJV above:

_____

_____

_____

_____

Memorize the verse and add it to your memory verses list.

Dear Heavenly Father,
Thank You for being merciful
and forgiving. We know that Your
Word tells us that You will forgive us if we
forgive others. Guide us by Your
Spirit to forgive.
Amen.

Reflection of Jesus

As Lord Jesus hung to a cross, beaten, bloody, bruised, in excruciating pain, nails pulling and throbbing through His hands and feet, He prayed for those that hurt Him.

"Father, forgive them, for they know not what they do."
Luke 23:46

Jesus asked God the Father to forgive those people, and even offered God an

explanation of why they hurt Him. In all of Jesus' suffering and pain, He thinks of the well-being of *others*.

Reflection of You

Ponder on the following verses, and add them to your memory verses list:
"For if you forgive men their trespasses, your Heavenly Father will also forgive you." Matthew 6:14

And be kind to one another, tenderhearted, forgiving one another, even as God in Christ forgave you.
Ephesians 4:32

Make a commitment to God to forgive others. Also ask *God* to forgive those that have wronged you. Ask God to help you see through the Holy Spirit's loving eyes, and also ask God to bless them:

Be thankful for someone who has wronged you. You will receive the amazing gift of sight from God – God will show you how He sees this person that you do not like. He will show you how this person is loved, and how God has a purpose for him/her.

Lesson 3:
It's All God's

Read *Genesis 50:19-26.*

Explanations in your reading:

> v. 20 "...to save many people alive..." People in Egypt and all around were spared starvation and death because Joseph was there.

> v. 24- Joseph leaves the earth assuring his family that God
> 26 is faithful. Joseph does not want them to give up on God's plan and God's will. God promised the land of Canaan (Israel) to Abraham, Isaac, and Jacob; therefore, one day they will go back. Joseph also insist they bury his bones there.

Write a summary and your own thoughts of the reading:

_____

_____

_____

• • • • •

Joshua 24:32 states,

"The bones of Joseph, which the children of Israel had brought up out of Egypt, they buried at Shechem, in the plot of ground which Jacob had bought...and which had become an inheritance of the children of Joseph."

Over 400 hundred years after Joseph dies, his bones are laid to rest in Shechem. It was in Shechem where young 17-year-old Joseph wandered looking for his brothers. And all of those years belonged to God.

In verse 19, Joseph gives all credit to God, once again, as he continuously did throughout his life.

To Potiphar's wife, Joseph tried to explain,

"How then can I do this great wickedness, and sin against

God?"

To the butler and the baker in prison, he explains to them,

"Do not interpretations belong to God?"

When the Pharaoh tries to praise Joseph for interpreting his dream, Joseph replies,

"It is not me; God will give Pharaoh an answer of peace."

and

"...God has shown Pharaoh what He is about to do."

and

"...the thing is established by God, and God will shortly

bring it to pass."

Joseph even named both of his children after what God had done: (41:51,52)

"...God has made me forget all my toil..."

"God has caused me to be fruitful..."

Joseph explains to his brothers in their bewilderment (42:18),

"...I fear God."

Joseph then explains to the brothers why they should not worry (45:5,7,8):

"...for God sent me before you to preserve life."

and

"...God sent me before you to preserve posterity for you in the earth, ..."

and

"So now it was not you who sent me here, but God; and He has made me a father to Pharaoh, ..."

After Israel's death, Joseph once again reassures his brothers (50:19, 20):

"Do not be afraid, for am I in the place of God?"

and

"...you meant evil against me; but God meant it for good, ..."

Joseph's entire life reflected good stewardship; that is, knowing and understanding that absolutely everything (and I mean everything); this book, this moment, this day, the breath you just took, the ability you have to read and see these words, the place where you are sitting, the warmth you feel, the coolness you feel, the screaming little sister or brother, whatever you may hear out the window, your parents, you, your future; it all belongs to GOD!

Do you think that maybe you can think of something that does not belong to God? Try. What, sin? Precious brother, if you have accepted Jesus Christ as your Savior, your sin has already been destroyed by God through Jesus Christ. God owns sin, too! God does not like it, and He did not create it, but He owns it!

For sin shall not have dominion over you, for you are not under law but under grace.

Romans 6:14

There is nothing about you that does not belong to God. I pray with all my heart that you never, never consume yourself with having more and more and more of the things of this world. God will provide you with more than an expensive sports car and a mountain chalet can ever give you.

...[God] is able to do exceedingly abundantly above all that we ask or think, according to the power that works in us.

Ephesians 3:20

I also pray that you never fall into the belief that you are too big of a sinner for God to do amazing things in your life. He loves you so much that if you were the only sinner in this whole world, Jesus would still go to the cross just for you. You are wonderful in God's holy eyes. Oh, and by the way, He owns you!

Look up **Galatians 2:20**, write it down, and hide it so deep in your heart that you cannot help but give God all the credit when you speak, just as Joseph did.

_____

_____

_____

_____

_____

Dear Heavenly Father,
Thank you for being my loving
God! Everything I am and everything
I have and everything I do is Yours. May
my goal in this life be to please You,
my Almighty God!
Amen!

Extra writing space for you:

Appendix

A. The Traveling Family
Genesis 46:6-27

The sons (and daughter) of Leah:

Reuben + 4 sons	=	5
Simeon + 6 sons	=	7
Levi + 3 sons	=	4
Judah + 5 sons (minus 2 that died) + 2 grandsons	=	6
Issachar + 4 sons	=	5
Zebulun + 3 sons	=	4
Dinah	=	+ 1
(plus Jacob)	=	**33**
		(verse 15b)

The sons of Zilpah:

Gad + 7 sons	=	8
Asher + 5 + 2 grandsons	=	+ 8
		16
		(verse 18)

The sons of Rachel:

Joseph + 2 sons	=	3
Benjamin + 10 sons	=	+ 11
		14
		(verse 22)

The sons of Bilhah:

Dan + 1 son	=	2
Naphtali + 4 sons	=	+ 5
		7

(verse 25)

All sons families added together:

33 + 16 + 14 + 7 = **70** people in all, as stated in verse 27. This shows the number of those from the house of Israel (Jacob) that lived in Egypt.

Verse 26 states that **66** people from the house of Israel traveled *with* Jacob: **70** total *minus* Jacob (**1**) = **69**.

69 minus Joseph and sons (**3**) = **66**.

(Joseph did not travel with them – he and his family were already there!)

B. Timeline of Joseph's Life

In Genesis 37, Joseph is seventeen years old. The past events of Abraham, Isaac, Jacob, and Esau have been told and are finished. God *wants* us to turn our attention toward Joseph for the remainder of the Book of Genesis. The following timeline is just to help you get an understanding of Joseph's age as God works in his life.

Through prayer, Bible-digging, and math, I completed this timeline. Therefore, these ages are my own calculations. I explain it further on my website, www.digginwithkaty.com.

<u>Event</u>	<u>Joseph's Age</u>
Joseph is sold as a slave.	age 17
Joseph worked for Potiphar (10 to 11 years).	age 17 to 26
Joseph is imprisoned (2 to 3 years).	age 26 or 27
Joseph interprets the baker's and butler's dreams.	age 28
Joseph begins to work for the Pharaoh.	age 30
Joseph oversees Egypt's 7 plentiful years, marries, and has 2 sons.	ages 30 to 37
The famine begins. Joseph oversees Egypt's 7 years of famine.	age 37

The brothers travel to Egypt, then   ages 38 to 41
back home bereaved, *back to Egypt*
a second time with Benjamin, then home,
and *back* to Egypt a third time with Jacob
and other family members
(no short trip, by the way).

Jacob, now 130 years old, sees his son Joseph.   age 41

The famine ends.   age 44

Jacob dies, and Joseph returns to Canaan   age 58
to bury his father.

Joseph enjoys time as a grandfather   ages 58 to 110
and great-grandfather in Egypt.

Joseph dies.   age 110

C. Memory Verses (NKJV)

The following verses are a compilation of all the memory verses from this study.

James 3:17a

But the wisdom that is from above is first pure, then peaceable, gentle, willing to yield, full of mercy and good fruits,…

1 Peter 3:15

Always be ready to give a defense to everyone who asks you a reason for the hope that is in you with meekness and fear.

Romans 11:36

For of Him and through Him and to Him are all things, to whom be the glory forever. Amen.

Jeremiah 29:11

For I know the thoughts that I think toward you, says the LORD, thoughts of peace and not of evil, to give you a future and a hope.

Colossians 3:23

And whatever you do, do it heartily, as to the Lord and not to men.

Proverbs 4:23

Keep your heart with all diligence, for out of it spring the issues of life.

1 Thessalonians 5:18

In everything give thanks; for this is the will of God in Christ Jesus for you.

Leviticus 26:12

I will walk among you and be your God, and you shall be my people.

Jeremiah 9:23,24

Thus says the LORD: "Let not the wise man glory in his wisdom, let not the mighty man glory in his might, nor let the rich man glory in his riches; v.24 But let him who glories glory in this, that he understands and knows Me, that I am the LORD, exercising lovingkindness, judgment, and righteousness in the earth. For in these I delight," says the LORD.

Ephesians 2:8, 9

For by grace you have been saved through faith, and that not of yourselves; it is the gift of God, not of works, lest anyone should boast.

206

Philippians 4:23

I can do all things through Christ who strengthens me.

Galatians 2:14a

But God forbid that I should boast except in the cross of the Lord Jesus Christ.

Mark 12:30

And you shall love the LORD your God with all your heart, with all your soul, with all your mind, and with all your strength.

1 Peter 4:8

And above all things have fervent love for one another, for love will cover a multitude of sins.

Proverbs 1:7

The fear of the LORD is the beginning of knowledge, but fools despise wisdom and instruction.

Isaiah 57:21

"There is no peace," says my God, "for the wicked."

Jeremiah 31:3

…Yes, I have loved you with an everlasting love…

Proverbs 12:22

Lying lips are an abomination to the LORD, but those who deal truthfully are His delight.

Ephesians 4:29

Let no corrupt word proceed out of your mouth, but what is good for necessary edification, that it may impart grace to the hearers.

Colossians 3:9

Do not lie to one another, since you have put off the old man with his deeds.

Psalm 19:14

Let the words of my mouth and the meditation of my heart be acceptable in Your sight, O LORD, my strength and my Redeemer.

Galatians 2:20

I have been crucified with Christ; it is no longer I who live, but Christ lives in me; and the life which I now live in the flesh I live by faith in the Son of God, who loved me and gave Himself for me.

Matthew 7:24

"Therefore, whoever hears these sayings of Mine, and does them, I will liken him to a wise man who   built his house on the rock."

Psalm 144:4

Man is like a breath; his days are like a passing shadow.

John 16:33

These things I have spoken to you, that in Me you may have peace. In the world you will have tribulation; but be of good cheer, I have overcome the world.

Isaiah 43:18, 19a

"Do not remember the former things, nor consider the things of old, behold, I will do a new thing."

2 Corinthians 5:17

Therefore, if anyone is in Christ, he is a new creation; old things have passed away; behold, all things have become new.

Philippians 3:13

...but one thing I do, forgetting those things which are behind, and reaching forward to those things which are ahead.

Proverbs 1:8, 9

My son, hear the instruction of your father, and do not forsake the law of your mother; for they will be a graceful ornament on your head, and chains about your neck.

Matthew 5:44

"...Love your enemies, bless those who curse you, do good to those who hate you, and pray for those who spitefully use you and persecute you."

James 1:19

So then, my beloved brethren, let every man be swift to hear, slow to speak, slow to wrath.

Hebrews 10:23

Let us hold fast the confession of our hope without wavering, for He who promised is faithful.

Philippians 3:20

For our citizenship is in heaven, from which we also eagerly wait for the Savior, the Lord Jesus Christ.

Romans 5:3,4

...we also glory in tribulations, knowing that tribulation produces perseverance; and perseverance, character; and character, hope.

D. Map

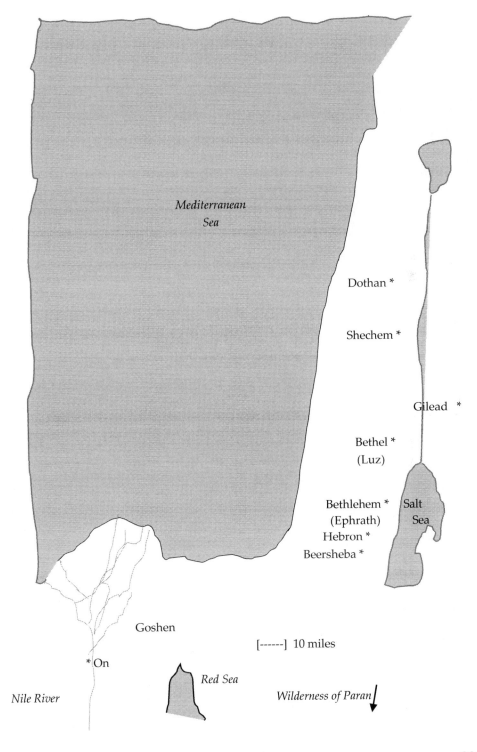

Mediterranean
Sea

Dothan *

Shechem *

Gilead *

Bethel *
(Luz)

Bethlehem *   Salt
(Ephrath)   Sea
Hebron *
Beersheba *

Goshen

[------] 10 miles

* On

Red Sea

Nile River

Wilderness of Paran ↓

Dear Reader,

God has placed the desire in both of our hearts to guide young people in understanding God's Word, applying His Word to their lives, and loving God with their all!

May we pray for you now? Dear Heavenly Father, You alone know the deep things of our hearts. And whatever may be there, You alone can make it better, and You still love us. I pray for the boy doing this study, that he gaze in awe and wonder of You, that he love You with all his heart, that he persevere throughout the years to see the plan You have for him. I pray that he fully surrenders to Jesus Christ, and shows courageous faith throughout his life. In the powerful name of Jesus, Amen.

All For Him,

Christopher and Katy Foster

About the Authors

Christopher and Katy Foster have three young children, Alex, Annabelle, and Ansley, and are strongly committed by God's grace to minister within their own family before giving priority to any other ministries. As members of Blackshear Place Baptist Church, they have remained compelled to serve and strengthen unity within the church family.

Katy Foster has been homeschooling her children for eight years. Her passion is to study God's Word and dig deeper into knowing His heart. Katy is also a Risk Reduction Instructor, in hopes to guide people loose from the deadly grips of alcohol and drugs. Although her books focus on boys and particularly her own son, she teaches growing *girls* God's truth at their home church.

Christopher Foster works as a middle school administrator, reflecting Christ as a father, a leader, and a man of God to students and staff. Chris enjoys reading history, and applying it to the Bible. His main focus is in his role as a husband and father, and is continuously leading the family in activities: camping, hiking, biking, exercising, healthy eating, gardening, movie nights, and much more. Chris is involved in the boys' middle school ministry at their home church.

More information and deeper digging into the lives of Joseph and David, as well as homeschool and spiritual insights, and are on our website. Please visit www.digginwithkaty.com.

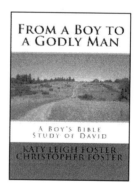

From a Boy to a Godly Man: A Boy's Bible Study of Joseph and From a Boy to a Godly Man: A Boy's Bible Study of David are available almost everywhere, including our website, and amazon.com.